Lives in Cricket: No 23

CW01072301

Brief Candles
McMaster, Hyland and Other One-Match Wonders

Keith Walmsley

First published in Great Britain by
Association of Cricket Statisticians and Historians
Cardiff CF11 9XR
© ACS, 2012
Reprinted in October 2012

British Library Cataloguing-in-Publication Data.
A catalogue record for this book is available from the British Library.

ISBN: 978 1 908165 14 5
Typeset and printed by The City Press Leeds Ltd

Contents

Preface

'Out, out, brief candle!
Life's but a walking shadow, a poor player
That struts and frets his hour upon the stage
And then is heard no more.'
Shakespeare: Macbeth

One of cricket's many delights is its ability to produce unlikely - some might say quirky - events which, though trivial, appeal to those of a certain cast of mind: a cast found perhaps disproportionately among cricket lovers.

Brief Candles celebrates the players involved in some of these more unlikely occurrences. More specifically, it tells of some of those who played in just a single first-class match, who were either unable to make an impression in their only chance or who did something special but were not given a second opportunity. Often, as we shall see, they were simply the beneficiary or victim of circumstances.

This book began as an attempt to write fairly full biographies of just two players: probably the most obscure Test cricketer, Emile McMaster, and the man with the shortest ever on-field first-class career, Frederick Hyland. With an eye to wider public interest, our series editor gently but wisely nudged me away from concentrating on just these two players. So how to expand the range of cricketers to be covered? Noticing that both McMaster and Hyland were, like me, born on the 16th of the month, and on a Saturday to boot, I wondered briefly if a whole book on cricketers born on Saturday 16th might have legs. Mercifully, I was quickly able to conclude that it didn't, even though some very famous cricketers share that birth distinction, among them Jack Hobbs, Stan McCabe and Heath Streak.

Instead I began to focus on a batch of 'one-match wonders' who, I felt, deserved more recognition for their admittedly limited exploits on the first-class cricket field. As well as detailing those exploits, I wanted to know how they came to be playing a first-class match in the first place, and why didn't they do so again. So that, in essence, is what *Brief Candles* is about.

The book falls into three parts. The first three chapters deal with 'those who didn't' - first-class cricketers who had only very brief on-field careers, such as McMaster and Hyland, together with several others who never had an on-field career at all. The next three chapters look at some of 'those who did' - players who, in their only first-class match, either scored a lot of runs, took a lot of wickets, or achieved some other memorable performance, only to disappear into cricketing obscurity once their match was over. Finally, there is a chapter on a cricketer who must, I suppose, be regarded at first-class level as one of 'those who didn't' but who has nevertheless spent – and continues to spend – a full and fulfilled 'life in cricket', and who as such makes a fitting conclusion to a book in the present series.

I have inevitably had to concentrate on British players, but I have also listed players from elsewhere with comparable, or near-comparable, one-match careers. If any reader has any further information about any of these players, or indeed about any of the Britons (and Irishmen) who form the main focus of the book, I would be delighted to hear from them.

Unlike other volumes in this series, the chapters that follow do not constitute full biographies of the players concerned. The sheer obscurity of several of them means that information on some key aspects of their lives, in or out of cricket, is lacking. So there are inevitably gaps, or unanswered questions, in the following pages. In particular I would have liked to be able to say more about the cricketing style of the players considered here, and about their on- and off-field character. But the passage of time and other circumstances mean that there is often little if anything available on these subjects. What I have found on them, I have sought to include; but I apologise if any reader feels that these aspects are inadequately covered. Please be assured that it is not for want of trying.

I also acknowledge that parts of several of the chapters may appear to fall into the trap of too many cricketing biographies by simply detailing players' performances match-by-match, or best-performance-by-best-performance. In mitigation, I plead that the unfamiliarity of the cricketers concerned means that this is necessary for an understanding of their cricketing skills and abilities, and for addressing the question of how they became first-class cricketers at all. I regret it if these sections read a little encyclopedically; but I make no apology for including them.

In putting *Brief Candles* together, I have had assistance from a huge number of people, most of whom I have contacted out of the blue and who have been only too willing to help in this project. Sadly there have been rather more than a few cases where attempts at contact have been made but not responded to; in particular, researching this book has brought home to me how little interest in, or awareness of, history there seems to be among some cricket clubs, which is a tragedy for those of us who like to delve into the game's past. But so it goes.

The most significant of the many positive contributions are gratefully acknowledged in a separate section towards the end of the book.

Reading, Berkshire
December 2011

Chapter One

The Unlikeliest Test Cricketer

Surely this can't be right – a cricketer who made his only first-class appearance in a Test match for England, was dismissed first ball, and didn't bowl, keep wicket, or take a catch in the field? The stuff of bad fiction, surely?

But it is true; the cricketer was J.E.P.McMaster, and he's there in all the standard reference books. So just who was this man, and what was he doing playing in a Test match?

Let's first agree on his name. In full it was **Joseph Emile Patrick McMaster**, and more than one reputable source – including, at the time of writing, ESPNcricinfo – has assumed that he was known as Joseph, or even Joe. But to call him Joe is akin to referring to two post-war England captains as Mike Cowdrey and Johnny Brearley: not only is the abbreviation out of place, but the name is in any case wrong. Joseph was indeed McMaster's first given name, but throughout his life he called himself, and was known as, Emile McMaster.[1] And it is as Emile that we will know him here.

So little about his life has been researched and published that not all that long ago it was possible for Joanne Watson to write this in her book *Moments of Glory*:

> Joe McMaster [hmm] made his only first-class appearance in a Test ... How he ever came to be included, with no apparent cricketing pedigree, isn't known. He may have been called upon just to make up the numbers'.[2]

It's time to make good this ignorance, and in so doing to answer the question: was Emile McMaster the most unlikely, and least qualified, Test cricketer of them all?

Ulster, Harrow and Cambridge

Emile McMaster was an Irishman. The son of a wealthy Ulster linen-mill owner, he was born in the town of Gilford in County Down, around 25 miles south-west of Belfast, on Saturday, 16 March 1861. The Gilford Mill was one of the largest in Ireland. At its peak in the 1860s it employed 1,500 people; and it made the McMaster family comfortably rich.

---

1. His death was registered, by one of his sons, in the name of 'Emile Joseph Patrick McMaster', and this same ordering of his names was given on some other occasions too. No birth certificate for McMaster has been traced - civil registration of births in Ireland was not required until 1864 - but the order 'Joseph Emile Patrick' is found in all the earliest available documents, such as on the Harrow School register, and in the 1881 census return, and there can be little doubt that this is the correct, formal, ordering of his forenames.

2. Joanne Watson, *Moments of Glory*, Lennard Publishing, 1990.

John Walsh McMaster, the mill's owner, and his wife, Mary Herron McMaster (née McKee), had 12 children, the oldest of whom, Hugh Dunbar McMaster (b 1843), inherited the mill on his father's death in 1872. Several of Hugh's younger brothers were also involved, one way or another, in the linen trade. But, apart from securing his privileged upbringing, linen seems to have played no part in the life of the seventh son, Joseph Emile Patrick.

The first we hear of Emile's youth is in September 1875 when, at the age of 14½, he enters Harrow School. Sadly no records survive that tell us anything of his character, or academic achievement, if any, during his time there.

But we soon learn that he played cricket. I have traced no certain record of any other members of his family being involved in cricket in Ireland, though an 'H.D.McMaster' is recorded as playing for the Gentlemen of the North of Ireland against the Gentlemen of Northumberland at Newcastle upon Tyne in 1867. This could well have been Emile's oldest brother; if so, we can imagine that Emile was probably brought up with family games of cricket on the lawns of Dunbarton House in Gilford. But there is no certain evidence for this.[3]

Whether his earliest cricket was in Ireland or at Harrow, by the summer of 1877 Emile was somewhere on the fringe of the Harrow eleven. Full records of the school's cricket at this time have not survived, so for details we must rely on secondary sources, notably *Scores and Biographies*. There we first read of 'E.J.P.McMaster' playing for the school in a twelve-a-side match against a strong I Zingari side on 30 June 1877. Only 16, Emile played alongside ten of the eleven who played for the school against Eton a fortnight later. He batted at No.12 and was bowled without scoring; but his bowling was effective in securing for the school a narrow first-innings lead (159 to 140), as in 57 balls he dismissed five IZ batsmen for 32 runs. All five had already played cricket at first-class level, so they were no easy touches. One of them, Spencer Gore, was just a fortnight away from the achievement that would immortalise him among followers of another sport: on 16 July 1877 he won the Gentlemen's Singles title at the first-ever lawn tennis championships at Wimbledon. Of tennis, more in a moment; but as a cricketer, Gore was less of a world-beater, and Emile was able to dismiss him for a duck.

So our first impression is that Emile was a bowler rather than a batsman. Regrettably, I have found no record that tells us anything of his bowling style. For some reason I imagine him bowling lobs, but I have no firm evidence for this one way or the other. On the other hand, there is reason to assume that he was a right-handed batsman: lefties were rare enough in those days for this to be remarked upon, but I have found no such remark in the few, later, references to his batting.

---

3   W.D.McMaster and P.G.McMaster, who represented North of Ireland against visiting English sides in 1867 and 1875 respectively, were not siblings of Emile, as he had none with those initials. But it is likely that they were members of his extended family.

His fine performance against I Zingari was not enough for Emile to force himself into selection for any of the three remaining games of Harrow's 1877 season. But he was back in the side at the start of 1878, scoring 0 and 0* respectively, batting last on each occasion, in matches against Mr E.E.Bowen's XI on 25 May,[4] and Oxford Harlequins on 8 June. His bowling, however, did not achieve the same success as previously. He took two wickets against Bowen's XI (again, both were first-class players, one of them – G.F.Vernon – a future Test player), but none against the Harlequins. He may not have been called upon to bowl in the latter game, as the visitors collapsed to 35 for six in reply to Harrow's 54 all out in this twelve-a-side match. One other oddity from these games deserves a mention: in the Bowen game, Emile took the one and only catch of his recorded career for the Harrow eleven, the batsman concerned being P.F.Hadow, who later that summer was to become the *second* winner of the Men's Singles at Wimbledon.

Whether through lack of success in these games, or injury, or the demands of study, or the appearance of more promising players, Emile did not play in any of Harrow's seven further recorded matches in 1878. And that was his last chance for a regular place in the school side, for he left the school at Easter 1879 – before the cricket term – to head to Cambridge.

You might think that, as a promising cricketer from Harrow School, Emile would have had a chance of making an impression on the cricket fields of Cambridge; but no. He went up to Trinity College in 1879 but did not play in the Freshman's Match at the start of the following summer, nor in any senior matches, let alone first-class matches, during his three years at the University. He wasn't even a regular in his college eleven. *The Sportsman* gives the scorecards of 20 Trinity matches during his three summers at Cambridge, of which Emile played in only six – one in 1880, two in 1881 and three in 1882.

In case his scoreless performances with the bat at Harrow and in his Test match conjure an image of a Chris Martin-like rabbit, I am pleased to be able to record that Emile produced a number of modestly useful scores in some of his matches for Trinity, the highest being an innings of 35* against Magdalene College in 1882. But here's an unexpected thing: he took no wickets in any of his three games in 1880 and 1881 – did he even bowl? He was, though, rather more active with the ball in 1882, taking ten wickets in his three games including five for 13 against Magdalene when, according to *The Sportsman*, he bowled 'remarkably well'. Meanwhile he was moving up the batting order, up to No. 5 in 1881, and even opening the batting in his last recorded match for Trinity, in June 1882.[5] So was he now seen mainly as a batsman who bowled a bit? As we shall see, that certainly seemed to be the case only a few years later.

If cricket wasn't occupying as much of his time at Cambridge as you might

4   Edward Bowen – coincidentally (or perhaps not) of Anglo-Irish extraction – was a housemaster at Harrow, where he taught from 1859 until his death in 1901.

5   That is, assuming that the batting orders given in *The Sportsman* can be relied on.

have expected, Emile was rising to the top in another sport. Harrovians had taken quickly to the new sport of lawn tennis – both Spencer Gore and Frank Hadow were Harrovians – and Emile too became a fine lawn tennis player: so much so that he was selected to represent Cambridge in the first-ever Oxford v Cambridge lawn tennis match, held at Prince's Ground, Chelsea on 24 and 26 June 1881. From the results of the match, Oxford had evidently taken even more expertly to the new game, and the Dark Blues won the doubles event on the Saturday by nine matches to love, with Emile, partnered by E.G.Watson, losing all three of his matches in straight sets. (All matches were played as best of three sets.) The singles on the rainy Monday were contested more closely, Oxford winning again, but only by a match score of 5-4. Emile lost his first match in three sets, but then secured a 7-5, 6-4 victory over T.P.D.Hogg, which according to *The Sportsman* featured 'some very fine play' on his part. He lost in straight sets in his final match, but overall could surely feel satisfied with his performance.

Nowadays participants in the Varsity lawn tennis match receive full Blues, but this award was not made to those playing in this very first such match. Even half-Blues were not awarded for tennis until around the time of the First World War, so sadly McMaster never received even that distinction for his efforts on court.[6]

He found time for some study too. In the summer of 1882 he obtained an ordinary BA degree, the course of studies for which mainly comprised the classical languages and mathematics, with a smattering of theology. He also cleared the path for a future career in law when in 1881 he was admitted to the Inner Temple. At Cambridge he took special examinations in law in both his second and third years, securing a humble fourth-class pass in 1881 but a second-class in 1882. His BA degree was conferred on him on 17 June 1882, and stayed with him for life; he did not later transform it into an MA, as those at certain universities were, and still are, able to do without further study.

He may have decided on the law as his career, but Emile was not yet inclined to settle down. He was called to the Bar in June 1888, and to do so he would have had to pass a wide-ranging examination, as well as 'keeping terms' by dining in Hall on a certain number of days over three years. Emile must have done all this; but he was by no means a full-time student of the law. Nor was he even a full-time resident in Britain. Ireland seems to have had no special hold over him, but his feet were itchy: as witness this chairman's introduction to a talk that McMaster gave at the Royal Colonial Institute in January 1902:

> Leaving England some fifteen or sixteen years ago, partly in search of health and partly in search of a country, the climate and prospects of which would be such as to induce him to make a home in it, he visited California, the Australian Colonies, and South Africa ... .[7]

---

6   We hear no more of Emile as a lawn tennis player. He never played in the Wimbledon Championships.

7   *Proceedings of the Royal Colonial Institute*, Vol 33 (1901-02), p 85.

So, somewhere around 1886 or 1887, Emile McMaster took a gap year, during which he made his first, and life-changing, visit to South Africa. When, a couple of years later, the opportunity of a further visit presented itself – and an opportunity moreover to combine the visit with his continuing love of cricket – he did not let it pass him by.

South Africa

The idea of an English side visiting South Africa to play cricket was first put forward in July 1888, when an item appeared in the magazine *Cricket* as follows:

> It is proposed to take out an English team of amateur and professional cricketers to the Cape Colony about the end of September. South African cricketers have for some time been desirous of meeting a representative English eleven ... . The management of the team is being undertaken by Major Warton, who recently served on the Staff in South Africa, from whom full particulars may be obtained on reference to him at the office of this paper.[8]

This is not the place to go into the details of the life of Major (later Lt-Col) Robert Gardner Warton (1847-1923), either as a military man (notably in Japan) or as an explorer (notably in Southern Africa), or into his qualifications to lead a pioneering tour to a new cricketing outpost. What is of particular interest from our point of view is the last sentence just quoted, which implies that those wishing to join the tour – particularly perhaps the amateurs – were invited to make themselves known to the Major, rather than being independently selected. An element of selection was no doubt still required; as Jonty Winch has written, 'there was, of course, some pressure on Warton to select those [amateurs] who could afford the tour'.[9] Some ability at cricket was undoubtedly a requirement too.

So what had Emile McMaster been doing to demonstrate this ability?

By the summer of 1888 he was back from his 'world tour' and, with the pressures of studying for his Bar exams lifted, he was able once again to devote himself to cricket. He was by now a member of MCC – he was first recorded as a member in 1886 – and in 1888 he played five times for them in matches against college and club sides in and around London. His name also appears in the scorecards of eight other matches recorded in *Cricket*, seven for a wandering side called the Ne'er-Do-Weels and one for another such side called the Peripatetics. And now he showed himself to be a batsman of fair club standard, and still a bowler as well, sometimes; as these performances indicate:

12 May:	46 for MCC v King's College, top score in 162 all out	
21 May:	48 for Ne'er-Do-Weels v Kensington Park, top score in a total of 133	
18 June:	43 for MCC v Pallingswick, top score in 212 all out	

8   *Cricket*, 12 July 1888, p 265.
9   Jonty Winch, *England's Youngest Captain*, Windsor Publishers, 2003.

23 June: 51 for Ne'er-Do-Weels v Henley, top score in a total
              of 204

11 July: 63 for Peripatetics v Ealing, top score in 157 all out;
              the next highest score was 17*

20, 21 July: eight wickets, five in the first innings, three in the
              second, for Ne'er-Do-Weels against Eastbourne; he
              also scored 24.

In the 13 matches in which he is known to have been involved in the summer of 1888, McMaster scored 356 runs at an average of 32.36, and took 16 wickets. In his five MCC matches he scored 122 runs at 30.50 and took one wicket.

With these cricketing credentials, and an affection for South Africa already in place, it is not surprising that Emile McMaster was one of the first to offer his services to Major Warton. And he clearly found early favour with the Major. On 23 August his name was included in an initial list of four professionals and three amateurs named for the tour,[10] and although the listed personnel changed a little in subsequent reports,[11] McMaster's name was always included.

Indeed, not only was he an early selection for the tour, but he made such an impression that before the tour started he was appointed as one of the members of the three-man Committee of Management for cricket matters on the tour, the others being the tour organiser, Major Warton, and the captain, Aubrey Smith.[12]

The tour itself lasted from 21 November 1888, when the ship carrying the tourists, *S.S.Garth Castle*, left Blackwall, until its return to London on 16 April 1889. McMaster joined the ship at Dartmouth on 23 November. The party that left in November was made up of twelve cricketers – six amateurs and six professionals – plus one 'social member', the mysterious A.C.Skinner.[13]   Between 21 December and 26 March they played 19 matches, all scheduled for two or three days. All but two of these games were played as 'odds' matches, their opponents fielding 15, 18 or even 22 players while Major Warton's side always stuck with 11.

Of the twelve bona fide cricketers on the tour, McMaster was the one rested for the first match; instead, he acted as one of the umpires. After that game one of the amateurs, J.H.Roberts, a Cambridge man whose only first-class match was a single game for Middlesex in 1892, had to return to England following the death of his mother. The team played a further seven games before his replacement – the professional George Ulyett – was able to join them. McMaster was therefore an automatic choice for these seven matches, but once Ulyett arrived McMaster and Hon C.J.Coventry usually alternated as the rested player. In all, he played in 13 of the 19 official tour

10   *Cricket*, 23 August 1888, p 361.
11   *Cricket*, 6 September 1888, p 393; *The Times*, 26 September 1888.
12   *The Cricketer*, 30 April 1955, p 121.
13   Skinner played in four of the tour games, scoring just one run and earning an ironic reference as 'England's greatest cricketer' in *Cricket*, 25 April 1889. At this stage I have been unable to discover any more about him.

games; Coventry, with 16 appearances, played the next fewest (apart from Roberts, Ulyett and Skinner), while four of the side – the amateur Monty Bowden and the professionals Maurice Read, Johnny Briggs and Arnold Fothergill – played in all 19.

The 'England' team which toured South Africa in 1888/89.
Back row (l to r): J.H.Roberts, J.M.Read, F.Hearne, J.Briggs.
Middle row: A.J.Fothergill, H.Wood (wk), R.G.Warton (manager),
C.A.Smith (capt), Hon C.J.Coventry, B.A.F.Grieve.
Front row: J.E.P.McMaster, M.P.Bowden, A.C.Skinner, R.Abel.

I do not propose to give a lengthy description of the tour – either its cricket, or the tribulations that the players experienced. These details can be found, if wished, in a number of other sources.[14] But for present purposes, Emile's tour deserves a slightly fuller description.

In his seven games before Ulyett joined the tour, McMaster batted 11 times, scoring 85 runs at an average of 9.44, figures roughly comparable over the same period with those of his fellow 'inexperienced' amateurs, Coventry, with 86 at 10.75 and B.A.F.Grieve, with 79 at 7.90. McMaster reached double figures four times, doing so twice in the match against XVIII of Kimberley, and reaching the heights of 34* against a South Western Districts XXII at Oudtshoorn early in 1889. But he also made three ducks, including a pair against the Cape Colony XV immediately after the game at Kimberley.

After missing the game in which Ulyett made his first appearance, McMaster

---

14   For example, in the contemporary volume *The Cricketing Record of Major Warton's Tour, 1888-89* published by C.Cox in Port Elizabeth in 1889 – in the absence of a stated author, this volume is referred to hereafter as '*Cox*'; in Jonty Winch's *England's Youngest Captain*, already cited; and in contemporary reports in *Cricket*. A useful quick summary of the tour is included in Peter Wynne-Thomas, *The Complete History of Cricket Tours at Home and Abroad*, Hamlyn, 1989. A limited edition reprint of *Cox* was issued by J.W.McKenzie in 1987.

returned with a score of 17 against XV of Natal at Pietermaritzburg early in February. But his batting had now peaked, and his remaining tour innings, in chronological order, were scores of just 4, 1, 0, 0 and 0.

Considering that he came on the tour with at least some reputation as a bowler, it is surprising that McMaster did not bowl a single ball in any of his 13 tour matches. The lion's share of the bowling was done by Johnny Briggs who took 293 wickets on the tour, at an average of just over 5; by Aubrey Smith with 134 at 7.4; and by Arnold Fothergill with 119 at just under 7. Between them these three bowled almost 90 per cent of the overs bowled during the tour, and took almost 93 per cent of the wickets;[15] but all the other members of the tour party, apart from McMaster and wicketkeeper Harry Wood, bowled on at least one occasion. Strange.

In all, his tour record in his thirteen matches was 17 innings, twice not out, and a total of 107 runs at 7.13, with a top score of 34*. He also took three catches plus one, or perhaps two, more when fielding as a substitute; and he did not bowl.

McMaster in resolute mode.

We can glean a little of his batting style from contemporary reports of tour games. He usually batted at eight or nine, dropping to ten on one occasion; but in two matches he went up the order, twice opening the batting (and being dismissed for one run on each occasion) and batting once at four (where he scored one run fewer). He does not seem to have been an aggressive or an overly confident batsman. More than once his arrival at the crease is followed in match reports by a statement to the effect that 'a succession of [four-ball] maidens followed' – there were as many as 17 in a row during his second innings in his first match. He seems also to have been an uncertain starter: he was dismissed first ball once on the tour, and second ball twice. And reports in *Cox* suggest that some of his run-scoring was a little fortuitous: 'he snicked him for a single'; 'he scored his first run by a pretty draw'; 'McMaster scored one off Grant, but had the field been alert enough he would not have got that run'. His running between the wickets also seems to have left something to be desired: 'McMaster went in only to run himself out by calling Hearne for an impossible run' and 'McMaster had a narrow shave of being run out in running a single for Briggs'.

But his batting was not all dawdling, flukes and hesitations. He hit two boundaries in his innings of 17 against Natal in February, and one in his innings of 10 against Kimberley in mid-January. He probably hit other boundaries during the tour, but they are not referred to in the match reports available. In particular, we have little detail of his innings of 34* against South Western Districts early in January. *Cox* tells us that it was

---

15   The statistics in this paragraph are based on the scorecards in CricketArchive as at February 2011. CA acknowledges that there are some minor discrepancies in some of these cards.

'carefully compiled', though *Cricket* called it an 'excellent' innings, and Jonty Winch refers to it as 'a fine innings'. We have no record of how long he batted for his 34*, or how his runs were made; but we do know that during it he shared in his highest partnership of the tour, one of 73 for the eighth wicket with Harry Wood, who scored 85 in all, during which, according to *Cox*, 'the field were kept hard at work leather-hunting'. However, as McMaster's share of the stand was, at best, 28, it would seem that most of the leather that required hunting was generated by Wood.

Indeed, McMaster was never the principal run-scorer in any of his partnerships on tour. His 107 runs were made while a total of 368 runs were being added, so his share while he was at the crease was barely 29 per cent – further evidence of the lack of aggression or domination in his batting.

One area that was not faulted was his fielding. *Cox* is not afraid to note occasional misses in the field, but attributes none to McMaster. He took only three catches during the matches in which he was one of the eleven, suggesting that he was generally an outfielder, rather than a close-to-the-wicket specialist. He also took at least one catch when fielding as a substitute.[16]

Of McMaster's role on the non-cricketing side of things, we know nothing. Circumstantial evidence suggests that he remained 'well in' with Major Warton: they are twice reported as travelling together on some of the many arduous coach journeys that were undertaken between the matches.[17] But there is no mention of him during the tour in his role as a member of the management committee, and neither does his name appear, either as speaker or as entertainer, in any of the reports of the tour's several social activities.[18]

Test cricketer

As the tour approached its end, McMaster could probably feel that he had not disgraced himself by his on-field efforts, even if he had hardly set the world alight. Two of the last three games were to be against more-or-less representative sides from all-South Africa – the only 11 v 11 matches of the tour. They have subsequently come to be accepted as the first-ever first-class matches in South Africa and, with significantly more reservations in a number of sources,[19] as South Africa's first Test Matches.

The first of the representative matches was scheduled for Port Elizabeth on 12, 13 and 14 March 1889. With all the playing members of the tour party available, there was little difficulty in picking the side. Nine selected themselves: these were the seven professionals, together with the captain

---

16   CricketArchive credits him with two sub catches in the game against XVIII of
       Durban in mid-February, but *Cox* gives the second of these to Frank Hearne.
17   Jonty Winch, *England's Youngest Captain*, pp 86 and 110.
18   As given in *Cox*, in Winch's book, and in David Rayvern Allen, *Sir Aubrey*,
       J.W.McKenzie 2005.
19   Notably by Rowland Bowen in *Cricket Quarterly* Vol 1 no1, and Vol 2 no 4, and
       in his book *Cricket: A History*, Eyre and Spottiswoode, 1970.

Aubrey Smith and vice-captain Monty Bowden. Basil Grieve had shown ability as an allrounder throughout the tour and so was a natural tenth pick, leaving the eleventh place between Charles Coventry and McMaster. As the former was currently in better batting form – his last four innings had been 9, 1, 18* and 10, against Emile's 17, 4, 1 and 0 – and had also had some success with the ball during the tour, it was fair enough that he got the nod. Five of the selected eleven – Abel, Ulyett, Read, Briggs and Wood – had already played for England against Australia, and were thus of bona fide Test standard, but the others had not and were not; and they never did, and never were. But this unrepresentative 'England' side – though not so named at the time – still won easily, beating 'South Africa' by eight wickets in mid-afternoon on the second day.

There followed another odds game in Kimberley (McMaster 0), succeeded in turn by the second representative game at Cape Town. Unfortunately Aubrey Smith had gone down with a fever immediately after the First Test, and was not able to travel to Kimberley. Although he had recovered in time to have played in the final game, he could not get to Cape Town before the match was due to start. So there was a gap in the 'England' side – and Emile McMaster was the only member of the touring party available to fill it.

Thus it was that, on Monday, 25 March 1889, the man from County Down took his place as one of the 'England' eleven in South Africa's second Test Match.[20] There was surely no fanfare to mark the occasion; the suggestion in one recent article that 'he was given his cap by the young England skipper, Monty Bowden' is simply ludicrous.[21] At the time it was just another tour match, albeit a specially important one; it was more than ten years before it gradually began to slip into the canon of Test matches, and so the suggestion that McMaster was formally 'capped' is nonsense. And in any case, the practice of Test debutants being physically presented with a cap by their captain just before the start of their first game is of very considerably more recent origin. Ah well.

The match itself took a predictable course. Bobby Abel (120) held firm in an 'England' total of 292, only Wood (59) otherwise getting beyond the twenties. Emile McMaster's entry into history came when Abel was dismissed with the score at 287 for seven, and he joined Grieve at the crease. The bowler was left-arm medium-pacer Gobo Ashley, also playing in his first and only Test. Abel had been his fourth wicket, and immediately McMaster became his fifth, caught at slip by Albert Rose-Innes off his first ball: 'smartly caught' according to *Cox*, but otherwise we know nothing of McMaster's brief innings.

After the visitors were all out, South Africa's two innings lasted a mere 75.3 four-ball overs between them, and 'England' won by an innings and 202 runs early enough on the second day for an unscheduled 'filler' match

---

20   Chronologically he was the fifth Irish-born Test cricketer and the first from Ulster, following T.P.Horan, and T.J.D.Kelly of Australia and L.Hone and T.C.O'Brien of England. There have been only five more since McMaster.

21   This comes from a fanciful article about McMaster by Richard Heller, entitled *The Hero of Zero*, that appeared in *Country Life*, 5 January 2006.

*Rare photograph of McMaster at about the time of his
South African cricket tour.*

- in which McMaster did not play – to be held.[22]

During his brief period as a Test fieldsman, McMaster did not take a catch, and there is no mention of him in the field in the contemporary reports that I have seen.[23] And that was that – his career as a Test cricketer all over in a day and a half.

In cricketing terms, the tour was regarded as a success, although early on there was concern when the visiting side lost four of its first six matches, which suggested to some in South Africa that they had been sent a weaker side than they had been hoping for. *Wisden* for 1890 has a credible explanation for the early lack of success: 'it is no libel to say that for a time generous hospitality had a bad effect upon the cricket'. It is reported that one banquet went on so long that none of the players had time to get to bed before the next day's cricket. The tour was certainly a very gruelling one: 'It was a case of travel, cricket, banquet, with no breathing time' (*Cricket*, 25 April 1889). But the players knuckled down after the first six games, and were unbeaten thereafter, winning 11 of the remaining 13 matches and having the upper hand in both the draws.

Cox includes a brief summary of the performances of each of the tourists. For McMaster, the verdict read: 'Mr Emile McMaster, moderate bat and fair field. Played in only thirteen matches during the tour and was fairly successful.'

Praising with faint damns, perhaps, but to judge from the figures, an accurate enough assessment of his performances.

Former Test cricketer

What next? Well, for the amateurs on the tour, the delights of South Africa clearly proved to be enduring. Smith and Bowden did not return home with the tour party; both played for Transvaal in the first-ever Currie Cup match in April 1890, and they also dipped their toes, unsuccessfully, into local financial affairs. When the *Garth Castle* set sail for home at the end of March, all the other amateurs, bar Skinner, had the intention of returning to South Africa at some time.

One to whom this certainly applied was McMaster, but first he had more important business to attend to in England. On Friday, 12 July 1889, in a civil ceremony at the Marylebone Register Office, he married Ethel Hancock. His wife, born in Shanghai, was the sister of the widow of one of Emile's older brothers, Percy Jocelyn McMaster (1852-1887).

McMaster and his bride were soon back in South Africa. Although there is

---

22   This game was not part of the official tour schedule, and so does not appear in most records of the tour. For what it is worth, the tourists batted first and made 248 (Bowden 82, Read 48; Skinner 0), and on the scheduled third day of the 'Test Match' South Africa had made 123 for six (A.B.Tancred 51) before the game was called off. The game was not taken very seriously. Major Warton played for the tourists, for whom most of the bowling was done by the batsmen; even Skinner bowled five, wicketless, overs.

23   Unfortunately the Cape Town newspapers for the relevant dates are missing from the newspaper library at Colindale.

no record of him playing further cricket, either in England or South Africa, he maintained an involvement in the game in his adopted country, for he is listed as one of the six men who umpired the first-class 'Champion Bat Tournament' held at Cape Town over Christmas and New Year of 1890 and 1891 – though who umpired which matches does not seem to be known.

Away from cricket, and from Cape Town, his principal occupation at first was the law, and he was engaged as junior counsel to Sir Henry Bale, the Chief Justice of Natal. But the high veldt of Natal had made a strong and lasting impression upon him, as summarised in this extract from a newspaper report of his death:

> While engaged in this legal work he laid the foundation of big business interests in the sugar-growing and tanning-bark industries, which later occupied his whole time, and with which he continued to be associated until his death ... Mr McMaster was one of the earliest to realise and exploit the highland plateaux of Natal, and quite recently he wrote ... for private circulation a most interesting book on the development of Natal, both in this direction and industrially. Mr McMaster had also written a good deal on cricket ... .'

Sadly I have been unable to trace any of these writings, or to discover their subject-matter.

The continuation of the above report then comes as a bit of a surprise, in the light of his – to put it kindly – dogged performances with Major Warton's side:

> As a contemporary of Abel and other famous men of the willow, he was a staunch adherent of forceful batting and an uncompromising critic of the more purely defensive modern tactics.'[24]

Well well!

It must have been during this period that he also earned for himself a reputation as a 'landed proprietor and planter in Natal', which is how he is described in J.A.Venn's register of Cambridge alumni,[25] but this description tells at best only part of the story of his time in South Africa.

His experiences in that country provided the foundation for the talk he gave to the Royal Colonial Institute in January 1902, as referred to earlier. Summaries of this talk, part geography lesson and part advertising pitch, were published round the world, and it can still be read on the internet today.[26]

Natal also saw the birth of two, and probably three, of Emile's children. Patrick Garnet Walsh McMaster (1890-1962) and Mary Ethel Josephine McMaster (1892-??) were both born in the McMasters' adopted town of Pietermaritzburg. His third child was Nora McMaster (1894-1979), who is

---

24   *Isle of Wight County Press*, 8 June 1929.

25   J.A.Venn, *Alumni Cantabrigiensis: 1752-1900*, Cambridge University Press, 1951.

26   The full text of the talk can be seen at www.archive.org/stream/proceedings17goog/proceedings17goog_djvu.txt. A summary of it was printed in the *Southland Times* in New Zealand, and is accessible online via http://paperspast.natlib.govt.nz

not recorded as a UK birth, and in the absence of any evidence to the contrary it seems reasonable to assume that she too was born in Natal.

But by May 1896 Ethel had returned to England for the birth of the last two members of their family, twins Humphrey (1896-1979) and Michael (1896-1965), born at Porlock in Somerset. And here the tale of McMaster's South African connections gets rather more cloudy.

We know that he, his wife and children (apart from Nora) were living in High Halden, near Tenterden in Kent, at the time of the 1901 census, and they were still at that address at least as late as 1903.

So, assuming that he was with Ethel in Somerset at the time of the twins' birth, was McMaster's return home in the mid-1890s a permanent one? If so, it seems that the South African interests that sustained him for the rest of his life were experienced at first hand for only some half dozen years. Whether the impending Boer War prevented him and his family returning to Natal is not known. Perhaps he returned to South Africa for a few more years after the birth of Humphrey and Michael, but certainly by 1901 he was back in Britain to stay – though not in Ireland. His direct connections with his homeland, and the family business, seem to have ended early in his life.

Although he described himself as a 'barrister-at-law' in both the 1901 and 1911 censuses, and remained on the 'Counsel' section of the Law List until 1921, he never practised law in England.[27] Indeed, by the end of the first decade of the twentieth century he had retired altogether and moved with his family to a comfortable, though by no means palatial, house called Afton Bank, on the edge of Freshwater on the Isle of Wight. This remained his principal home until he died, although at least some of the time he also maintained a London address at Montagu Street, off Portman Square.[28]

On the island, of which he was very fond, Emile was a member of the Yarmouth Town Trust and of the Solent Yacht Club, though we have no record of whether he actually sailed. The notice of his death in the local newspaper also tells us that he was 'a billiard player of far above the average amateur standard'.

But cricket seems to have continued as his first sporting love. In retirement he frequently visited London, combining his business activities with cricket-watching. And although he may only have become a Test cricketer retrospectively, it seems that he was almost certainly aware that he held this distinction,[29] for on his death the report in the *Isle of Wight County Press* – surely compiled by his family – referred to him as 'an old player of international repute'.

The same source states that he did not enjoy very good health in his later years, 'although he made a remarkable recovery from a serious operation

---

27   I am grateful to Michael Frost of the Inner Temple Library for this information.
28   See for example the notice of the marriage of his son Michael in *The Times*, 25 May 1920.
29   *pace* Martin Williamson, *The ignorant internationals*, article on ESPNcricinfo, dated 28 November 2009

about three years since'. It was on one of his visits to London, on Friday, 7 June 1929, that Emile McMaster died suddenly at the Whitehall Hotel[30] in Guilford Street, Bloomsbury,[31] the cause of his death being recorded rather graphically as 'heart failure; exhaustion; duodenal ulcer; suppression of urine'. He was 68 years old, and died less than a week after his erstwhile competitor for a place in the 'England' cricket team, Charles Coventry, who was his junior by six years.

Emile McMaster was buried in Highgate Cemetery on 11 June 1929. His grave today bears no inscription and is hard to find, its southern end being obscured by a box tree, and the adjacent grave having ridden over it on its western side. A sad and anonymous end for, in cricketing terms, an almost anonymous player.

Legacy

Before finally passing on to an assessment of McMaster's worthiness as a Test cricketer, a word is called for about the not inconsiderable sporting legacy he left to his three sons.

The oldest, Patrick, sometimes called Pieter, was a military man who ended his career with the rank of Major. He received the OBE for his military services during the First World War and was 'a Kenya settler of distinctive personality with an unusual talent for games and sports'. According to his obituary in *The Times*,[32] he played representative cricket in Kenya as well as being a good golfer and shot, and an outstanding angler. He was described as 'a really great judge of cricket' who had been watching a match from the pavilion at Lord's on the afternoon of his death.[33] This obituary also includes the intriguing statement that Patrick played cricket as a fast bowler for Hampshire before the First World War. Unfortunately I can find no corroboration for this. He certainly did not play for Hampshire at first-class level, and his name does not appear in the few Club and Ground scorecards that found their way into the local press during the years leading up to the war.

Emile's twin sons, Humphrey and Michael, both went into the Royal Navy and both reached the rank of Lt-Commander. Both were outstanding golfers in South Africa and in Britain, Humphrey playing in the British Amateur Championships in both 1928 and 1929. Michael also excelled at squash, winning the South African Amateur Championships in 1926 and 1927, and reaching the last eight of the British Amateur Championship in 1929. After leaving the Navy, both became directors of the sports equipment

---

30   In 2011, the Whitehall Hotel was a youth hostel going by the name of 'Smart Russell Square'; it appeared to be in good external repair, but inside it looked run-down and well past any glory days it may have experienced in the 1920s.

31   The coincidence of his life beginning and ending at Gilford/Guilford has not escaped me, but does not seem worthy of comment beyond this note.

32   On 1 June 1962. This obituary is the source of much of the material, and all of the quotations, in this paragraph.

33   It is tempting to think that this may also have been true of his father. There was certainly a match on at Lord's on the day of Emile's death, and we already know of his custom of watching cricket during his visits to the capital; but on this we can only speculate.

firm Slazengers Ltd, Michael serving as chairman and managing director from the 1930s to the 1950s.

Although both twins followed their father in also playing cricket, it was Michael who had the stronger record. It was surely a proud moment for Emile when, in May 1920, Michael equalled his father's achievement by playing in a single first-class match, for the Navy against Cambridge University at Fenner's. He did rather better than his father, scoring 7* and 6, batting at nine in the first innings and six in the second, and taking one for 55 and none for 18. He opened the bowling in the first innings and bowled Gilbert Ashton for seven. Another in the Cambridge side in this game was J.C.W.MacBryan who, four years later, would make his own record-breaking minimal impression on Test cricket by becoming the only cricketer who never batted, bowled, or kept wicket in his entire Test career.

At least Emile McMaster managed better than that.

The unlikeliest?

The time has come to put McMaster's Test career into some context.

In terms of its brevity:
- he is one of only 21 players whose Test careers ended on the day after they started (exclusive of those whose match had only one or two playing days, but where play would have taken place on additional days if the weather had permitted)

- measured by the total length of his match in overs, at the equivalent of 132.4 six-ball overs McMaster had the joint third-shortest career of any Test cricketer, behind Jack MacBryan at 66.5 overs and Ali Naqvi at 132.2

- measured by the length of time he was actually on the field, 304 balls, McMaster's was the shortest of all Test careers, apart from those of two players, Andy Lloyd 37 balls and Greg Loveridge c 42 balls, who retired hurt early from their only Tests

- he is one of only five batsmen to be dismissed by the only ball he faced in Tests. The others were England's E.J.Tyler, Australians Roy Park and Bill Hunt, and South African Gerald Bond.

In terms of his performance:
- he is one of just over fifty cricketers who batted but never scored a run in their entire Test careers

- he is one of only 15 players who batted but did not participate in a single run – either their own or their partners' – in their entire Test careers: that is, the only partnership/s they were involved in were runless

- he is one of only seven players who did not score a run, or bowl, or keep wicket, or take a catch, in their entire Test careers

- he is one of only three players (the others are George Hearne and Percy Twentyman-Jones) who are common to both the last two bullet-points, and thus one of only three Test cricketers who batted but did not score or participate in a run, and who in addition did not bowl, or keep wicket, or take a catch, in their entire Test careers.

These facts help to explain and perhaps to justify why McMaster is so little remembered today, except by lovers of cricket's esoterica. The fact that only two other players can lay claim to comparable 'performances' under all of the bulleted topics indicates that his may fairly be regarded as one of the least influential Test careers of all.

But the most unlikely, and the least qualified?

There have been several Test cricketers whose selection at that level may be regarded as 'unlikely'. This unlikeliness may derive from:
- the player's inexperience prior to selection, for example, Douglas Carr or D.C.H.Townsend; or

- the moderate nature of their first-class records, for example certain amateurs selected as tour captains, such as R.T.Stanyforth, Harold Gilligan, or the 1936 Indian captain the Maharajkumar of Vizianagram; or

- their good fortune in being in the right place at a time of 'crisis' in the main squad, for example Ken Palmer, Tony Pigott, Neil Williams or Brandon Bess; or

- the dubious Test status of the matches they played in, such as the nineteenth-century Tests in South Africa; or

- the fact that the regular Test team was unavailable and so some second-stringers had to be drafted in, for example, for Australia in the first Melbourne Test of 1884/85, or for several countries during the Packer rift of the late 1970s.

Some players will fall into more than one of these categories, but for my money none has a better qualification under more categories than does Emile McMaster. He had no first-class experience before going on tour, he was only drafted into the 'Test' side for want of anyone better when it became clear that the tour captain was not going to be able to get to the ground on time, and his 'Test' was definitely one of dubious status. Add to that the fact that his form in the matches just before his 'Test' appearance had been conspicuously poor, and I find unavoidable the conclusion that Emile McMaster was the most fortunate, very probably the most undeserving, and – yes – the most unlikely Test cricketer of all.

But let not that diminish his glory. Emile McMaster is an established member of the pantheon of Test cricketers, a place to which many millions of players and followers of the game would aspire. He deserves our respect, not our only-half-joking scorn, for reaching that height.

Chapter Two

Of the Late Frederick J.Hyland, again

An awful lot of cricketers have played only a single first-class match. As at mid-2011, as many as 90 have done so without either batting or bowling.[34] What marks **Frederick James Hyland** out from the other 89 is firstly, the extreme shortness, 12 balls, of the match that constituted his entire first-class career and secondly, the fact that 43 years later his brief moment in the spotlight was the subject of a light and wistful essay in Ronald Mason's delightful book *Sing All A Green Willow*.[35]

By that time, Hyland's life was over. Indeed, what prompted Mason's essay, which he entitled simply 'Of the Late Frederick J.Hyland', was the appearance of his four-line obituary in *Wisden* 1965, with its reference to the extreme brevity of his first-class career. Mason's thesis was 'by whatever curious mistake of fortune ... the distinction that he can wave in the teeth of all competitors is an indisputable and proud one. He had played first-class cricket; and what kind of proportion of genuine cricket-lovers can say the same?'

Mason did not seek to explore the facts behind Hyland's brief career, or the story of the man himself, commenting: 'for the purposes of these meditations I do not need to know [these details]; he remains for me an epitome of the life of man as illuminated long ago by the Venerable Bede, the sparrow flying into the banquet-hall, fluttering for a moment in the light and heat, and then flying forth at the far door into wintry darkness'.

And of course he was right: none of these details really matters. But Hyland's sheer obscurity has fascinated me for some time. How come this Sussex man played for Hampshire? Did he have any cricketing pedigree at all? Or was he perhaps spotted wandering round the ground at Wantage Road one rainy day in June 1924 and invited, regardless of any cricketing ability, or any county qualification, to make up the numbers in a depleted Hampshire side?

To my mind, more prosaic than Ronald Mason's, these questions needed answering. And when I found that Hyland shared a birth-date (same date, different year) with Jack Hobbs, another thought arose. Was he, by contrast with The Master, a great unfulfilled talent who, but for the appalling weather of June 1924, might have embarked on a long and distinguished first-class career?

---

34   Thirty of the 90 at least participated in the game by keeping wicket; all but five of these 30 got their names on the scorecard by recording a dismissal. (One of the five non-dismissers was Bob Richards, qv). Of the other 60, 14 took at least one catch, but the remaining 46 appear on the scorecard solely as 'did not bat'.

35   Ronald Mason, *Sing All A Green Willow*, Epworth Press, 1967.

So I set about looking for some answers.

Origins

The Who's Who of Cricketers, published for the Association in 1993, tells us that Hyland was born on 16 December 1893 at Battle, near Hastings in Sussex, died at Hartford in Cheshire on 27 February 1964, and that he was a lower-order batsman who played as a professional in one match for Hampshire in 1924. His *Wisden* obituary in 1965 adds a note on the brevity of his one first-class match, and concludes with a sentence that inspired some of Ronald Mason's speculations: 'Hyland later earned a reputation as a nurseryman in Cheshire.'

Following up the sources that have assisted in the preparation of all the chapters in this book – local newspapers, census returns, certificates of birth, marriage and death, family history websites, other internet-based sources, and a huge range of sources spinning off from all of these – we find that only some of the above facts are true. Even some of the more detailed sources, such as the obituary placed (presumably by his family) in the *Northwich Guardian* edition of 5 March 1964, do not bear the closest examination.[36] But what follows is the result of checking and cross-checking all sources, and should, I hope, be accurate and reliable.

His date of birth of 16 December 1893 is substantiated by his birth certificate. Fred, as he was known, was the seventh of nine children, and the third son of five, born to George and Frances Annie Hyland, who certainly lived in the registration district of Battle, but not in the town itself. Changes over time in the parish boundaries have confused the picture somewhat, but Fred was actually born in the village of Sedlescombe, about 2½ miles north-east of Battle. In 1893, the family home where he was born, known variously as Orchard Place or Orchard Cottage, was actually in the parish of Westfield, but physically it was and is clearly a part of Sedlescombe, and to say that he was born in Westfield (as his birth certificate implies) actually misleads to the tune of about two miles.[37]

In the nineteenth century a number of Hyland families, no doubt related, lived in and close to Sedlescombe, but none was in any way affluent. Fred's father was an agricultural labourer and sometime gamekeeper on the adjacent estate owned by the artist and landowner Hercules Brabazon.[38] The family had some local celebrity, not to say notoriety:

> In the later 19th century, Orchard Cottage was occupied by the Hylands, father and son. Both had been inveterate poachers, the father having got shot in the leg for his pains. George, the son [Fred's father] followed his father's example so expertly that Squire

---

36 This obituary appears to have formed much of the basis of a feature on Hyland by Neil Jenkinson in the Hampshire C.C.C. Yearbook for 2003, but here too, not all the details fully check out.

37 The parish boundary has since been changed, and Orchard Cottage is now firmly within the parish of Sedlescombe.

38 The estate, known as Oaklands, is now home to the Pestalozzi International Children's Village, an educational charity set up for children from developing countries to live and study.

Combe decided that the only way to cure him was to make him his gamekeeper. Thus Orchard Cottage became the gamekeeper's. To walk past it on Mrs Hyland's baking day was a mouth-watering experience, for she was famed in the village as a most perfect baker. Their sons were all expert at sports and one [Fred] played for his county. The only one to remain in Sedlescombe returned there badly gassed after the First World War, but he still managed to play cricket for many a year.[39]

The village cricket pitch is now only about 200 yards from Orchard Cottage, but in the nineteenth century it was a little further away within the Oaklands Estate. I have been unable to find any definite evidence of any Hylands playing cricket for the village team in the days when Fred was a child, but this surely was where he and his brothers were first introduced to the game.

On the move

Despite the family's firm Sedlescombe roots, Fred, like many an estate worker of the day, was regularly on the move throughout the first part of his life. In the 1911 census he turns up a long way from home, as an under-gardener at Sandon Hall near Stafford. By the outbreak of the First World War he had headed back south again. When he joined up in November 1915 his address was given as The Cedars Gardens in Harrow Weald, north-west of London; yet when, three months later, he was discharged from the Army 'having been found physically unfit for further war service' (the *Northwich Guardian* obituary says that he did not see active service because of a knee injury), his intended place of residence is stated to be at Leyswood Gardens, Groombridge, near Tunbridge Wells.

Around 18 months later he was back in the London area. On 23 September 1917, at Holy Trinity Church, East Finchley, just across the road from the Summers Brown factory that supplied Jack Hobbs with his bats, Fred Hyland married local girl Ada Olive Gwendoline Flucke.[40] On the marriage certificate his address is now given as Addlestone (in Surrey), his occupation as gardener.

Four years later, he was living in Ringwood in Hampshire: and this is where his cricketing story really starts.

Cricket in Hampshire, and further afield

The year 1921 saw the birth of Hyland's daughter Beryl, and his first rise to some prominence in local cricket. From at least mid-June of that year he began appearing regularly in the Ringwood eleven, as a specialist bowler;

---

39   Beryl Lucey, *Twenty Centuries in Sedlescombe*, Regency Press, 1978.

40   The striking surname set me off trying to find a family link between Fred Hyland and Diana Dors, née Diana Fluck [sic], but without success. Ada's family came originally from Herefordshire, though Ada herself was born in London, and Diana Dors in Swindon. Incidentally, Ada's maternal grandmother bore the maiden surname of Trumper; but once again I can find no link to a certain more famous person of that name.

a return of five for 25 against Lymington on 2 July no doubt helped to seal his place in the side. His younger brother Ernest played alongside him in some of these matches; indeed, a number of members of both Fred's and Ada's families made their homes in this part of Hampshire around this time, one of them being Fred's mother who lived locally until her death at Ernest's house in nearby New Milton in 1936.

By no means all local matches were reported in detail in the local press at the time, and even when they are, reports and scorecards tend to concentrate more on the performances of the batsmen than of the bowlers. Fred Hyland, despite his description in the *Who's Who*, definitely came into the latter category. In the matches for which scores are reported in either the *Hampshire Advertiser* or the *Bournemouth Echo*, he almost always batted with the tail-enders and rarely scored more than a handful. But wickets he took in numbers.

By far his most memorable performance came in a twelve-a-side match against Lyndhurst on Whit Monday, 21 May 1923. On their home ground at The Carver, Ringwood scored 107, Hyland contributing eight, and then bowled out their opponents for 23, Hyland taking nine wickets for eight runs, including a hat-trick and six wickets in seven balls. The report and scorecard in the *Bournemouth Echo* only give the details of the dismissals of eleven Lyndhurst batsmen, so we don't have full information, but at least five of Hyland's wickets were 'bowled'. Such was the Lyndhurst collapse that batsmen numbers five to twelve managed just one run between them.

On its own, such a performance was unlikely to get Hyland noticed at higher levels. But over the 1923 season as a whole his figures were consistently impressive. He topped the club's averages with 91 wickets at 6.99 apiece, off 375.5 overs with 61 maidens, taking almost as many wickets as the next three wicket-takers put together.

The die was cast when, at the end of the season, Hampshire C.C.C. decided they needed to look more closely at their local talent. The club's minute book for 14 September 1923 records that, 'at Sir Godfrey Baring's suggestion it was decided that all recognised cricket clubs in the county should be asked to advise the Secretary of any very promising talent among the players, especially of any promising bowler'.[41]

This surely was how Hyland came to the attention of the county club. With his fine record in 1923, and by now an undoubted residential qualification for Hampshire despite his Sussex origins, he was asked to play in a trial match at Northlands Road at the start of the 1924 season.

At this point, things get a little murky. The match was played on 3 May 1924, but the report of it in the *Southern Daily Echo* makes no mention of Fred – which makes it a little surprising to read in the same paper a

---

41   From the Hampshire CCC Minute Book for 1921-1931, now held at the County Record Office in Winchester, under reference 10M89/92. Baring was a vice-president of the club.

month later that Hyland 'did quite well' in this game.[42] The *Echo*'s match report does however remark on the bowling of one Needle, 'who took four wickets for 21 runs' in the trial game.

And then one looks at the scorebook,[43] which shows 'J.F.Hyland' as a did-not-bat, at twelve in the order, for Alec Kennedy's side and, at first sight, as taking just one wicket (Brown b Highland [sic] for 4), while Needle has, indeed, four. But for two of Needle's victims (Newman and Boyes), the name 'Hyland' has been written, spelled correctly and in a different hand from the rest of the card, above the original bowler's name 'Needle'; and in the bowling analysis, Needle is now given figures of only two for 21, while Hyland's are raised to 8-2-34-3; not a bad three victims either. In addition, 'Highland' also caught out Tennyson. If these details are right, and it seems reasonable to assume that they are the correction of a case of mistaken identity by the original scorer, then Hyland had indeed done 'quite well' in the trial match.[44]

He was now firmly in the county's mind. So when, just over a month later, Ronnie Aird, W.G.L.F.Lowndes and Alec Bowell were all unavailable for the match at Northampton due to start on 11 June, their places went to three of the less experienced players from the trial match. These were opener Thomas Smith, who had appeared in eight previous county matches in 1923 and 1924; and first-class debutants Norman Bowell, son of Alec, and Hyland, reported by the *Southern Daily Echo* as 'a right-hand medium-pace bowler from Ringwood'.

Although over 30 years old, he was in the side on merit, albeit a little fortuitously. And so he turned up at Wantage Road on the morning of Wednesday, 11 June, to take his place in the side of his adopted county, alongside the likes of Lionel Tennyson, George Brown, Philip Mead, Alec Kennedy and Jack Newman.

But 1924 was one of the wettest summers of the twentieth century.[45] Two county matches due to start in May had already been abandoned without a ball bowled, and the round of fixtures starting on 11 June was another to be decimated by the weather. Of the nine first-class games scheduled for 11 to 13 June, only five got under way on the first day, and only one of these, at Dudley, where around 70-75 overs were bowled, had anything approaching a full day's cricket. There was no play in five of the games on the scheduled second day, and similarly none in five (but not exactly the same five) on day three. Just one of the nine matches ended in a definite result, and in only one of the other eight games were both first innings

---

42   In the newspaper's report on 10 June 1924, just ahead of Fred's first-class debut match. The same words appeared in the same paper the following day, this time without the qualifying word 'quite'.

43   County Record Office, ref 10M89/3.

44   But if the original scorer was right, perhaps Hyland made his first-class appearance under false pretences: but no, we can't countenance that!

45   The third wettest, after 1931 and 1912, according to the article *Cricket Season Weather, 1890-1993* by David Jeater in *The Cricket Statistician*, 89 (Spring 1995), pp 26-29; and the second wettest, after 1903, according to the essay *1903 - The Wettest Summer of Them All?* by John Kitchin in *Wisden* 1986, pp 77-80. The differences result from the different locations chosen by the authors as their sample sites.

completed. In all, 12 out of the scheduled 27 days play in these matches were completely lost, with the games at Leicester and Bath both being abandoned without a single ball bowled; and on only eight of the other 15 days did the weather relent sufficiently for as many as 100 runs to be scored in the game in question.

Northampton suffered as badly as anywhere. 11 June began with heavy overnight rain, with sharp showers following at intervals. Shortly before the scheduled start at midday another downpour ruled out any prospect of play before lunch. An inspection at 2 pm concluded that there was little chance of play before 4 pm, but an inspection at 3.30 pm brought more positive news: play would start at 4.30 pm if there were no more rain. This was good news for the 'large number of spectators [who] had been waiting outside the gates, and a goodly company inside the ground'. The toss was made at 4 pm. Northants won and decided to bat; whereupon heavy rain promptly began to fall, and the prospects of any play receded once again.

Nevertheless, sunshine followed and allowed a further inspection at 4.50 pm, which in turn led a decision to start at 5.20 pm if there were no further rain. One further delay held things up for 25 minutes before finally at 5.45 pm, 'amid a cheer from the very patient spectators', the teams took the field, umpire John Moss (or perhaps his partner Arnold Warren) called 'play': and Fred Hyland became a first-class cricketer.

An ominous black cloud was hurrying towards the ground as Alec Kennedy bowled the first over to William Denton from the Football Ground end. The first ball reared awkwardly, but Denton played through five dot-balls before a misfield in the slips off the sixth ball allowed the batsmen to take a single. Jack Newman bowled a maiden to Denton from the other end, and then, as the players were taking their positions for the third over, and as Denton's partner Dick Woolley was preparing to face his first ball, heavy rain began to fall yet again. So that was it for the day.

And for the match too. Things looked promising on the morning of Thursday 12th, when there was bright sunshine until rain began half an hour before the scheduled start of play at 11.30 am. An early lunch was taken, with good hopes of a prompt resumption thereafter; but at 1.50 pm, or according to another source, just after lunch (perhaps they liked long lunches at Wantage Road) there was heavy rain for a quarter of an hour. The umpires inspected again soon after the rain stopped, and at 2.20 pm called off play for the day. The pattern of events on Friday 13th (!) was similar: heavy overnight rain, no play before lunch, an inspection soon after lunch, and abandonment at 1.45 pm.[46]

So Fred Hyland's first first-class match lasted twelve balls, probably well under ten minutes, and yielded just one run. As a new boy in the team, it seems unlikely that he would have been fielding in the slips, so it was probably not he whose misfield led to that run. Indeed, he may very well not have touched the ball at all.

---

46   The descriptions of play and non-play in the preceding paragraphs have been assembled from the reports in contemporary editions of the *Northampton Daily Chronicle*, the *Northampton Daily Echo*, and the *Southern Daily Echo*.

The sparse details of Hyland's first-class career recorded in the
Hampshire scorebook of 1924. The names of the visiting team
were not listed in the scorebook at all.
(Courtesy of Hampshire Record Office.)

But he was beyond question a first-class cricketer.

Hyland was named in the twelve for Hampshire's immediately following
match at Trent Bridge, but Ronnie Aird was now once again available,
and in a batsman-for-bowler swap Aird replaced him in the team; surely
a little harsh, as both Thomas Smith and Norman Bowell were principally
batsmen, and one of them would have been more of a like-for-like change.[47]

Evidence suggests that Hyland travelled with the team to Trent Bridge,
and indeed stayed with them for another week. On Wednesday, 18 June,
he played at Northlands Road for the Hampshire Hogs against Harborne,
taking five for 31 in Harborne's first innings; and on 19 June he went
with a full Hampshire first-team to Newport to play a twelve-a-side match
against the Isle of Wight. Hampshire, or two of their players at least, seem
to have taken this game pretty seriously: Kennedy and Newman bowled
unchanged in the island's first innings of 94, and then opened the batting
together in Hampshire's innings. Hyland was finally given a chance to bowl
when the island batted again, after Hampshire had declared at 235 for five
(Hyland dnb), and he took one wicket as they reached 67 for five before
the game ended.

And that seems to have been that for Fred Hyland's county career. The
county were back to full strength for their next Championship match on
25 June at Portsmouth, and I have not traced any further record of him
playing at anything approaching this level thereafter. We do, however, have
records of how much he earned from his brief flirtation with the county

---

47   The game at Trent Bridge was Smith's last first-class match, and Bowell's
      last for Hampshire. The latter played his third and final first-class match for
      Northamptonshire in a non-Championship match in 1925, as noted in Chapter
      Five.

game: ten shillings for playing in the trial match early in May; £1 10s 0d for representing the county at Northampton,[48] plus a further £1 10s 0d expenses; £7 for the Notts match, and 12s 8d for the match at Newport, plus 12s 8d expenses, giving a grand total of £11 15s 4d (£11.77).[49] Not bad for eight days' work, especially when six of them were spent doing virtually nothing at Northampton and Nottingham.

So there was no county engagement for him for the rest of 1924, despite ending the season once again as Ringwood's leading wicket-taker, with 45 wickets at 7.13.

In Ringwood, for the first time we have evidence of Hyland working on his own account, as a fruiterer, florist and landscape gardener with his brother-in-law Robert Flucke in a firm unambitiously named Hyland and Flucke. Their partnership was dissolved in March 1924, though Robert continued to trade as a fruiterer in Ringwood for some years after that; maybe Fred, from his previous experience, had been purely the landscape-gardening component of the partnership?

1924 was to be Hyland's last season with Ringwood, for by the following season he was on the move again. Perhaps if he'd stayed in Hampshire the club would have kept him in mind if they were once again briefly short of available players. But his peripatetic nature meant that he had now given up, for ever, any chance of a fuller first-class career.

According to his obituary in the *Northwich Guardian*, between 1925 and 1928 Hyland played for Norfolk and for Broughty Ferry, in Scotland. I have been unable to corroborate the latter: he is certainly not referred to in the official handbook for Forfarshire CC, the principal club based in Broughty Ferry, for 1926. But by the end of that year he had indeed moved to Norfolk, for in early August 1926 he is reported by the *Eastern Daily Press (EDP)* as fielding 'very well indeed' as substitute for the county in a Minor Counties Championship game against Kent II at Lakenham.[50] From 1927 he played regularly for East Dereham, generally taking a fair few wickets for them, including five for 25 against Norwich School in July, and five for 28 against CEYMS in August.[51]

Fred Hyland in his forties, unidentifiably capped.

If he had moved to Norfolk directly from Ringwood in 1924 or 1925, he

---

48   The usual match fee for a capped professional player was £8, but for such an abbreviated game an uncapped player could hardly expect such riches.

49   Details from the Hampshire C.C.C. Match Expenses Account Book, held at the County Record Office, ref 10M89/65.

50   His first known game in Norfolk was on 17 July 1926 when he played for East Dereham against Norfolk Wanderers in a match advertised as for Hyland's benefit.

51   As well as playing for East Dereham, Hyland also played one match in September 1926 for the South Norfolk club, an appearance which suggests he was close to being selected for the Norfolk side.

would have been qualified to play Minor Counties cricket for Norfolk from 1927. If, on the other hand, he spent some time in Scotland before reaching Norfolk, he would have had to wait two years before being qualified by residence for his new county. Either way, in May 1928 we find him playing in a Norfolk county trial match at Lakenham, in which he scored 12, one of his highest recorded scores (!), and took one for 49 in 15 overs, bowling 'well but without the best of luck', according to the *EDP*. But this was not enough to get him in the county side for the 1928 season; and by 1929 he had moved on again, for one final time.

One last move

The first 35 years of Hyland's life saw him living in seven different places, or eight, if he did indeed go to Scotland. But the move he made to Cheshire in late 1928 proved to be his last, as he spent his remaining 35 years in or very close to the town of Northwich. He was tempted there by the offer of a job as the groundsman and playing professional for ICI at their Winnington Works just north of the town. He, Ada, Beryl and their son Kenneth, who had been born at Ringwood in July 1923, joined in due course by Philip, born in Northwich in April 1932, settled initially at 10 Moss Terrace, a house that looks out straight across the bowling greens and cricket ground of the Winnington Park club. Later they moved the short distance to 149 Beach Road at Hartford, in an area that today has a quiet, middle-class, suburban feel to it. Fred Hyland had come a long way from his early days as a poacher's son in rural Sussex.

With a secure job and a growing young family, Hyland now finally put down his roots. Based on the match reports printed in the *Northwich Guardian*, he regularly played and umpired (not in the same game!) for Winnington Park in matches in the Manchester Association. At first their star bowler, his performances on the cricket field seem to have fallen away after the 1929 season; but he had other sporting activities to keep him occupied, for he also represented Winnington Park at hockey, bowls and billiards.

Off the field of play he was an even busier man.

For a start, he was committed to his role as ICI's groundsman. He looked after two grounds, Winnington Park Recreation Ground and Moss Farm, and under his stewardship both had reputations as among the best-maintained grounds in the county. He trained to become an expert in turf preparation, and the quality of the squares he tended is still recalled today by older members of the local sporting community. As well as preparing pitches for competitive 'external' matches, he was responsible for the pitches used in the ICI Works knock-out competition, at a time when 20,000 people worked there. With each department fielding a team, 'the quality was high and the competition fierce'.[52] In the winter he tended the hockey pitches at Winnington Park.

---

52   Like so much of my information on Fred's activities in Cheshire, this quotation comes from a personal communication from Mike Talbot-Butler, doyen of the Cheshire County League and of many other sporting activities in Cheshire, and an erstwhile acquaintance of Fred Hyland, to whom I am greatly indebted for his wide-ranging assistance.

He also had a sideline as a repairer of cricket and hockey equipment. Mike Talbot-Butler recalls that he may also have been a cricket-bat maker; at any rate, he was certainly very wise about bats. This despite the fact that, on his own admission, he had a low (and apparently accurate) regard for his own batting.

Away from the regular sporting field Hyland maintained other competitive interests, in horticulture and in cage birds. According to his *Northwich Guardian* obituary, 'his sideboard became full of cups and trophies, won all over the country for showing chrysanthemums, and his prize-winning budgies and canaries also brought him fame.' Indeed, it was the latter that earned him his only entries in the pages of *The Times*, other than his listing in Hampshire's team-sheet in 1924: on 1 February 1934 he was named as a 'leading winner' in the Norfolk Canaries class at the National Show of Cage Birds at the Crystal Palace. At the Norfolk Bird Show in November 1935 his buff hen won the cup for the best amateur's Norwich plainhead.

There is no reason to doubt the reference in his *Wisden* obituary to him having a reputation as a nurseryman, even though its source is unknown; but whether this reputation derived solely from his success with his chrysanthemums is less certain. Neil Jenkinson's piece on Hyland in the 2003 Hampshire Yearbook tells of him opening a market garden where he specialised in orchids, though I have been unable to trace where this was. And although in his will Hyland described himself as a 'retired market gardener', this was evidently not such a prominent element of his life as to justify a reference in the family-written obituary in the *Northwich Guardian*. For us to think of him now, on the strength of one line of *Wisden*, only as a successful nurseryman is, at best, telling only a small part of his story.

For there was yet more. During the Second World War he served as an ARP warden, and also during the war, if not earlier, he gave his name to another venture with which his family was long associated in Northwich. The local telephone directory for 1945 has an entry for 'F.J.Hyland, Pet Stores' at 11 Crown Street, and that entry was retained until 1959, by which time Fred was 65. Whether Fred was active in running the shop alongside his full-time duties for ICI in the earlier part of this period is not certain; if he ran this shop for the best part of 15 years, it is surprising that it is not referred to in the *Northwich Guardian* obituary. We know that he resigned his post with ICI early in November 1951, for reasons given as 'personal betterment';[53] maybe he wanted to spend more time with his pets, or was this the start of his later-life career as a nurseryman? From 1960, the directory entry for the shop changes to 'K.P.Hyland, Pet Stores' – K.P. was his son Kenneth, known as Ken – and in 1966 the store moves from Crown Street to 9 Market Hall, as Hyland's Pet Stores. By now, or soon after, both of Fred's sons had become involved in the business, with Philip, a leading light of the local angling community, diversifying the business by adding the sale of fishing tackle to the core pet business.

---

53   Information from his personnel records at ICI, kindly supplied in a personal communication from Judith Wilde of Brunner Mond, predecessors of, and successors to, ICI at Winnington in June 2009.

A move of the store to Applemarket Street followed in 1983, but around this time a double tragedy struck, as both of Fred's sons died young in the early 1980s – Philip in January 1982 at the age of 49, and Ken in April 1983 aged 59, little over a month after retiring from the pet shop. Both had married, but I have not traced any male descendants and I believe that the Hyland family name has now died out in this line.

Sadly, the family's pet shop has long since vanished; I suspect it closed around the time of Ken Hyland's retirement. There is a pet shop today in Northwich's main shopping street, but although the name of Hyland Pet Stores still rang a bell with the proprietor when I visited in May 2010, it has no connection with the Hyland establishment.

Fred Hyland had died before the family tragedies of the early 1980s. He saw out his last years apparently as the owner, or at least the occupier, of three properties. As well as the house in Beach Road, he also retained ownership of 10 Moss Terrace, and there are references both in telephone directories and in the memory of Mike Talbot-Butler to a further property in the village of Goostrey, a few miles east of Northwich. In some years in the 1960s there are separate phone-book entries for Fred's widow both at 149 Beach Road, Hartford, and at Woodstock, New Platt Lane, Goostrey; Mike's memory is of Fred living in Goostrey at nearby Booth Bed Lane. Maybe his peripatetic tendencies didn't leave him in his later years, after all: they were just focused on a smaller area.

Hyland celebrated his 70th birthday just before the end of 1963, but it would seem that he was by now ailing. In mid-February 1964 he made his will, leaving both his properties, 149 Beach Road and 10 Moss Terrace, to Ada, and almost all the rest of his estate ultimately to his three children. He died less than a fortnight later on 27 February at his home

Fred Hyland lived here in Beach Road, Hartford, Cheshire at the end of his life. Photograph taken in 2010.

in Beach Road, the cause of death being recorded as mitral stenosis, a heart valve disorder, with influenza and bronchitis as secondary factors. He would probably have been poorly for some days if not weeks before his death, with shortage of breath and coughing fits well before this. He was cremated at Altrincham Crematorium on 2 March; there is, sadly, no memorial where his ashes were scattered.

So passed the man with the shortest first-class career of them all. With his only match lasting a mere twelve balls, Fred's career as a first-class cricketer was less than a quarter the length of his nearest rival to this title (and that rival may well remove himself from the list in time):

Shortest first-class careers, by number of balls bowled in the match

Overall

Balls			Achievements
12	F.J.Hyland	Hampshire v Northants, Northampton, 1924	did not bat or bowl
50	D.Cleaver	Central Districts v N Districts, Napier, 2010/11	wk: no dismissals
59	Abdur Rehman	} Baluchistan Gov's XI v Sri Lanka 'B', Quetta, 1988/89	did not bat, bowl or field
59	Mohammad Asad		did not bat, bowl or field
60	A.Judson	Yorkshire v Kent, Sheffield, 1920	bowled 1 over for 5 runs
78	Mushtaq Nazir	} Gujranwala v Sheikhupura, Muridke, 2002/03	scored 3*
78	Zeeshan Amin		scored 11*
78	Kaleem Imran	} Sheikhupura v Gujranwala, Muridke, 2002/03	wk: 1 stumping
78	Kashif Imran		did not bat or bowl

In Britain

Balls		Achievements
12	F.J.Hyland	Hampshire v Northants, Northampton, 1924	did not bat or bowl
60	A.Judson	Yorkshire v Kent, Sheffield, 1920	bowled 1 over for 5 runs
105	C.Lawrence	MCC v Notts, Lord's, 1898	did not bat or bowl
312	E.Slinger	MCC v Oxford University, Oxford, 1967	scored 12*; 1 ct
385	N.G.R.Mair	Scotland v Worcestershire, Worcester, 1952	scored 4*
401	R.J.Richards	Essex v Jamaica, Leyton, 1970	wk: no dismissals

In the County Championship

Balls			Achievements
12	F.J.Hyland	Hampshire v Northants, Northampton, 1924	did not bat or bowl
60	A.Judson	Yorkshire v Kent, Sheffield, 1920	bowled 1 over for 5 runs
422	J.Coulthurst	Lancashire v Northants, Manchester, 1919	did not bat, bowl or field
474	E.Wakelin	Worcestershire v Essex, Bournville, 1910	scored 6
499	H.Longland	Northants v Lancashire, Manchester, 1907	did not bat or bowl
541	A.J.Ricketts	Somerset v Surrey, Taunton, 1936	did not bat or bowl

Assessment and memories

In terms of the questions raised at the start of this chapter, we have established that Fred Hyland's appearance for Hampshire was entirely legitimate in terms of the qualification rules; that he most certainly had a respectable cricketing pedigree, though as a bowler rather than as a batsman as implied by the *Who's Who of Cricketers*; and that, equally certainly, he was not just making up the numbers on the team-sheet at Northampton.

In addition, we must also conclude, sadly, that he cannot be regarded as a great unfulfilled talent at first-class level. He had one outstanding season at club level in 1923, and came into the Hampshire side the following year on the strength of a good performance in a trial match. But he was by now already in his thirties, and was not able to reproduce the same form consistently thereafter; and when, a few years later, he moved to Norfolk he was not able to force his way into their Minor Counties side, though admittedly at the time Norfolk already had a 'varied and effective' bowling attack, according to *Wisden*. So even if it hadn't rained in Northampton in mid-June 1924, it seems most unlikely that that game would have been the start of a long and illustrious first-class career.

So much for Fred Hyland, cricketer. But thanks to Mike Talbot-Butler, we also know a little more about him than just the bones of his life and his several careers: from Mike's recollections we learn something of Fred Hyland the man.

Mike knew him when he (Fred) was in his mid-50s, and remembers him as a man of about 5 ft 11 in and stockily built, with powerful, hairy arms. He found him easy-going and humorous: apparently he liked to pull Mike's leg. Despite their age difference, he talked freely with Mike, speaking with what Mike assumed at the time to be a Hampshire accent, but which he acknowledges may well have been a Sussex rural accent. Although Fred talked happily about county cricket, he did not talk with Mike about his former involvement in it. (Although from his *Northwich Guardian* obituary and the article in the 2003 Hampshire Yearbook it seems that his family and contemporaries, just like Beryl Lucey in Sedlescombe, knew that he was a former county cricketer, though they did not necessarily know just how short his career had been.) Of his playing style, Mike recalls that from what Fred told him, he likened him to Alec Bedser in pace. But his batting was not up to much.

Mike also met Ada, briefly; his abiding memory is that she made him some nice cups of tea – an excellent quality in a wife, though I say so myself.[54]

* * * * *

Each year on 16 December, the Master's Club lunch is held at The Oval to celebrate the life and achievements of Jack Hobbs on his birthday. And in the evening of that same day, if you chance on the right restaurant in North London you will find a small group of friends having their own Master's Dinner, in celebration of the birthday and the memory of the man who stands for all first-class cricketers, major, minor, or mini-minor: the late Frederick J.Hyland. For as Ronald Mason concluded, 'Of his kind is the game given its enduring strength and fascination'.

After nearly 50 years, Mike Talbot-Butler's memories of Fred Hyland are understandably a little hazy. But the words he uses to sum him up show that the man whom Mason chose to stand for all first-class cricketers is fully worthy of our admiration as a man, as well as our respect as a cricketer: '[he was a] lovely man, whose brief acquaintance I have always valued.'

I rather think I would have liked the late Frederick James Hyland.

---

54   Ada Hyland survived Fred by 18 years; she died in hospital near Northwich in September 1982, aged 92.

Chapter Three
Never Seen

At least Fred Hyland was on the field for a couple of overs. There are around a dozen even less fortunate players, whose one and only first-class 'appearance' was spent wholly in the pavilion, or even away from the ground altogether. Yet they are quite properly classed as first-class cricketers because they were members of a side in a match that was started, even though bad weather or some other unlikely circumstance conspired to prevent them setting foot on the field at all.

This unfortunate turn of events is known to be the case for the twelve listed in the table below, though the last two at least may have further opportunities.

First-class cricketers who never set foot on the field of play

W.Hunt	English Residents v American-Born	Nicetown	1882
T.J.Hearne	Middlesex v Philadelphians	Lord's	1908
J.Coulthurst	Lancashire v Northamptonshire	Manchester	1919
P.Herbert	Gentlemen of South v Players of South	The Oval	1920
Abdur Rehman	Baluchistan Governor's XI v Sri Lanka B	Quetta	1988/89
Mohammad Asad	Baluchistan Governor's XI v Sri Lanka B	Quetta	1988/89
P.Imadura	Moratuwa v Sinhalese	Colombo	1989/90
Qamar Saeed	Faisalabad v Islamabad	Islamabad	1993/94
B.Ludidi	Easterns v Free State	Bloemfontein	2004/05
H.B.Ilangaratne	Kurunegala Youth v Singha	Kurunegala	2006/07
M.L.A.Fernando	Sinhalese v Colombo	Colombo	2009/10
K.Nagan	KwaZulu-Natal v Easterns	Benoni	2009/10

The seven listed below may have missed out in the same way, but the evidence examined so far is not conclusive.

First-class cricketers who possibly never set foot on the field of play

J.N.Dudlow	Kent v Nottinghamshire	Nottingham	1841
J.B.Mill	Hampshire v MCC	Lord's	1842
G.F.B.Mortimer	Surrey Club v MCC	Lord's	1852
J.T.Griffiths	Nottinghamshire v Gloucestershire	Clifton	1891
P.G.Peiser	Rhodesia v Transvaal	Bulawayo	1922/23

| Kapoor | United Provinces v Northern India | Delhi | 1935/36 |
| R.Malhotra | Jammu and Kashmir v Railways | Delhi | 1959/60 |

Two of the three instances in England in the first table, those of Hearne and Herbert, were one-offs, where the circumstances of their non-appearances were decidedly out of the ordinary. We'll meet these two a little later. For now, let's concentrate on the other English instance, in which the circumstances that conspired to prevent our man entering the field of play were a little more 'normal'.

The Unlucky Oddfellow

For Lancashire, as for most other county sides, 1919 was a season for rebuilding. Three of the players who had appeared in their County Championship side in 1914 had been killed in the war, and a number of other long-serving players had reached the end of their county careers. Only three of those who played in Lancashire's last Championship match of 1914 also played in their first match of 1919.[55] As the season progressed Lancashire, like several other counties, found difficulty in establishing a settled side. Only four men appeared in 20 or more of their 24 Championship matches, and only another half-dozen appeared in more than half their matches. In all they used 27 players in the Championship season,[56] only five of whom had played more than half of the county's matches in 1914, and eleven of whom had played no first-class cricket at all in 1914. Ten of these eleven made their first-class debuts in 1919; the other made his Lancashire debut in that year, having not otherwise played at first-class level since 1906.

This latter was Vic Norbury, a Hampshire-born all-rounder who had appeared 11 times for his native county in 1905 and 1906. In 1912 he became the professional at East Lancashire, which is Blackburn's team in the Lancashire League. It was above all on the strength of his League performances that he was selected for Lancashire's first postwar Championship match. These performances included 100 wickets in 26 single-innings matches of 1912, and 109 in 1913; as a batsman he still holds the East Lancashire club records for most runs and most centuries by a professional.

Norbury came close to another century of wickets in the 1919 Lancashire League season, but another East Lancashire bowler was now out-performing him. As Norbury's county form fell away towards the end of the season, it was this man, **Josiah Coulthurst**, known as 'Jos' or sometimes 'Josh', who replaced him in the Lancashire eleven for the final game of the season, at Old Trafford against Northamptonshire. This was a two-day game, as were all Championship matches in 1919, starting on Wednesday 27 August.

On that first day, Lancashire won the toss and batted, but incessant

---

55   To be fair, only three others in the 1919 XI were making their Lancashire debuts.

56   Again to be fair, I should record that they used 28 players in their 26 games of 1914.

rain prevented play until 4.30 pm. At this point 'the conditions were more suitable for football than cricket, [with] a strong, cold wind',[57] and Coulthurst was probably glad to be able to spend the day in the pavilion, trying to keep warm. When play finally started, the soft wicket was of no great help to the visitors' bowlers, and Lancashire reached 198 for six in the 70.2 overs possible before play ended just before 7.30 pm. Coulthurst, listed at eleven, was no doubt hoping for better things on the second day.

But no. On 28 August, only the West Country escaped a full day of heavy rain. Games at Bristol and Taunton were able to resume briefly, and just long enough at Taunton for Surrey to knock off the runs they needed to defeat Somerset. But there was no play at all in the day's three other first-class matches, at Lord's, at Southampton, and at Old Trafford. Unceasing heavy rain caused Lancashire's game to be abandoned during the lunch interval, when it became clear that there would be no chance of a resumption; and so ended Lancashire's season, and Jos Coulthurst's first-class career. Perhaps he trod the Old Trafford turf before the game started on the Wednesday; maybe he even ventured on to it in the rain on Thursday. But he never had the chance to do so in anger during the three hours of actual play in the game.

So who was Jos Coulthurst, and how had he forced his way into the Lancashire side for this game? And why did he not make up for his disappointment – I presume he was disappointed at the turn of events at Old Trafford – by gaining selection in a later season?

Blackburn's finest?

Born in Blackburn on Christmas Eve 1893, just eight days after Fred Hyland's arrival 250 miles to the south-east, Coulthurst showed his promise early. He joined the East Lancashire club as a teenager in 1907 or 1908 (sources vary) after playing a single game in the local Sunday School League, and moved rapidly from the third eleven to the seconds, where he played regularly before making his first eleven debut at Rawtenstall on 30 May 1914. His quick left-armers brought him one for 27 that day, although according to the local paper he would also have had the wicket of century-maker, and future Lancashire player, Alfred Pewtress 'if the fielding had been up to concert pitch'.[58] However, he had not established himself in the first eleven by the time the Lancashire League was suspended at the end of the 1916 season, playing only very occasionally for the firsts in 1914 and 1915, and not at all in 1916.

He had offered his services to the war effort in the previous year, but was rejected on account of defective eyesight. Re-examined in September 1916 he was accepted and joined the Army Service Corps (later the RASC); within two months he was in France. His enrolment papers show that the 22-year-old Coulthurst stood 5ft 7½ in tall, weighed 11st 10lb, and wore glasses to help correct his eyesight.

---

57   *Manchester Guardian*, 28 August 1919.
58   From an article on Coulthurst by 'Nomad' that appeared in the *Blackburn Times*, 12 July 1919. This article is also the source of all the extracts quoted in the following four paragraphs.

As a clerk (whose overall standard the Army classed as no better than 'fair', with poor typewriting and no shorthand), he appears to have escaped being sent to the front. Indeed, cricket seems to have been as much a part of his war as was his contribution to the fighting, and he took full advantage of the opportunities available. He is reported as taking 93 wickets at an average of 3.72 for the 'Annexe J' team in France, though whether this was over a single season or over his entire Army career is not clear. He also played for the garrison side at Le Havre, alongside such players as H.D.G.Leveson Gower and John Daniell, and sometimes against an Australian services team that included the likes of Sgt-Major Warwick Armstrong.

Coulthurst did not join up until September 1916, so presumably he was available for East Lancashire for the greater part of that season. But he did not play in the League that year. The club had recruited off-spinner Jonathan Brooks, the professional from Ribblesdale Wanderers, a Clitheroe-based club in the already-suspended Ribblesdale League, who played as an amateur in 1916 because the Lancashire League did without professionals for that one season. In 24 matches Brooks took 119 wickets for the club, still the club record for an amateur, and the second-best tally by an amateur in the League's history. When the war ended, Brooks chose to return to the Wanderers. Thus, following his demob early in 1919, Coulthurst found himself an automatic member of the East Lancashire attack, which was described at the time as being 'only of a weak character' – Norbury apart, presumably. He had chosen to return to his home-town team despite offers from other clubs, including Rishton and Church, and a good decision it turned out to be.

Although now a regular in the first eleven, Coulthurst began the 1919 League season appearing short of confidence, and 'more workman than artist'. His first four matches brought him only eight wickets, but as his confidence grew so did his tally of wickets, with 37 in his next seven matches, including four six-fors and one seven-for.

With Lancashire looking to strengthen their county squad, a trial game was to be held at Old Trafford on 28 July. By now Coulthurst had taken 72 wickets in the League at an average of 9.23, and his club were riding high in the league table, so it was no surprise that he was invited for a county trial. In 12 overs he took three for 37, Neville Cardus, no less, in the *Manchester Guardian* describing his bowling as follows:

> left arm and fast, [he] kept up a good pace for quite a long time, bowling very few loose balls. Now and then he tried a slow one, but his action gave the batsman warning. Surely the most difficult problem in the world for the bowler is to conceal his pace variations; the more one finds cricketers attempting this art and failing, the more one realises the greatness of George Lohmann.[59]

Cardus regarded the bowling in this game as 'very much below the level of the batting in point of the refinements which give the impression of county class ... little of it had even a suspicion of the spin and variety which

---

59   *Manchester Guardian,* 29 July 1919.

are essential against first-rate batsmen'. Nevertheless, Coulthurst had done enough, and was continuing to do enough in the League, to justify selection for a second trial match on 18 August. This time he opened the bowling; he began with a bang, dismissing three batsmen before a run was scored. His final figures were four for 26 off 11 overs, with three of his victims out bowled.

It was this performance above all that secured his place in the county side to play Northamptonshire a week later. A merit selection surely, especially as since mid-May he had been consistently outbowling Norbury in League matches, not by much, but consistently; and Norbury himself was having an unhappy time for Lancashire, with five single-figure scores in his last eight innings, and a bowling return over his last five innings of only two for 140.

What happened next, as far as Coulthurst's first-class career is concerned, has already been described. At League level, however, he and his club were achieving new heights. On 6 September, in the needle match with fellow title-chasers Nelson, Coulthurst reached his 100 wickets for the League season; apart from the exceptional case of the 'amateur' Jonathan Brooks in 1916, he was the first amateur ever to achieve this landmark for East Lancashire, and only the sixth amateur to do so in the League's history. (Again, this excludes instances in the exceptional season of 1916.)[60] And when, a week later, East Lancashire beat Colne while Nelson were losing at Ramsbottom, the Blackburn club had won the Lancashire League for the first time in their history[61] to great local rejoicing. Their tally of 19 wins in 26 matches remained a League record until 1975.

The lion's share of the club's success was down to the bowling of Coulthurst, who ended with 101 wickets at 9.78, and Norbury, with 98 wickets at 10.98. Coulthurst himself later recalled that 'Vic Norbury and I bowled almost unchanged that season,' and he was not far off the mark: between them they accounted for over three-quarters of the overs bowled for the club, and took over 80 per cent of the wickets. Norbury and Arthur Dawson, both with 870-odd runs at around 40, were the only batsmen to shine, although even non-batsman Coulthurst[62] had his moment of glory when, with a straight-batted 13*, he helped to add 27 for the last wicket to secure a vital one-wicket win over Accrington as the season approached its climax late in August.

Cricket after Old Trafford

If Coulthurst could repeat and build on his 1919 successes, and if he wanted it, a longer first-class career was surely there for the taking. But sadly he couldn't, and he didn't.

---

60   To this day, and again excluding 1916, it has only been done eleven times.

61   East Lancashire also won the championship of the North-East Lancashire Cricket League, forerunner of the Lancashire League, in 1891; some sources regard this as akin to winning the Lancashire League. But certainly, at the time the 1919 success was regarded as a 'first' for the club.

62   He admitted to such a description himself. So little is known of his batting that it is unclear whether he batted right- or left-handed. It probably made little difference either way.

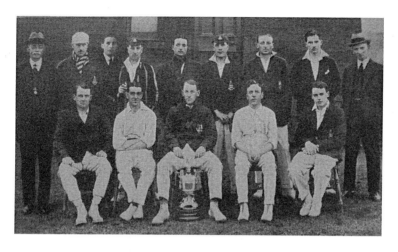

The East Lancashire side which won the Lancashire League in 1919.
Standing (l to r): T.Eastwood (secretary), J.W.Carmichael. T.Turnbull, A.Dawson,
D.V.Norbury, J.Coulthurst, E.Higham, R.C.Bardsley, J.Campbell (chairman).
Seated: T.K.Stones, R.Mercer, H.Emmett (capt), S.J.Catterall,
J.Turnbull. Norbury was the club professional.

At the end of the 1919 season he was approached by another unnamed Lancashire League club to turn professional, but he turned the chance down as he had 'no ambition in that direction'.[63] He also resisted any blandishments to make himself available for the county side, deciding that his business commitments meant that he could not devote the necessary time to three-day matches.[64]

But in any case, his outstanding form of 1919 now deserted him. In 1920 'weather conditions were not favourable to Coulthurst's bowling',[65] and he took only 42 wickets as East Lancashire slipped to a disappointing ninth place in the League. Although he continued to take wickets steadily for the club over the next ten years, this, and his figure of 46 wickets in 1922, were to prove his highest wicket tallies in any year after 1919. That's not to say that he didn't have his moments, among them his only League hat-trick against Haslingden in August 1921 at Blackburn's Alexandra Meadows ground, and his career-best figures of eight for 14 against the same opponents in the away fixture the following May. But these were only fleeting glimpses of his triumphs of 1919.

By the 1929 season, Coulthurst could see that his Lancashire League days were coming to an end. He played only once for East Lancashire in that year, and in July dropped down to the Ribblesdale League to make a single appearance for Ribblesdale Wanderers, taking three for 43 against Darwen. For 1930 he stayed in that league, but moved a little closer to home to play

63   *Blackburn Times*, 13 September 1919.
64   As reported in Coulthurst's obituary in the *Blackburn Times*, 9 January 1970.
65   From 'A history of East Lancashire Cricket Club' in East Lancashire CC, *Souvenir Handbook of the Merrie England Bazaar ... March 1929.*

for Whalley, who had won the League title the previous season, for the first time since 1913.

With 26 wickets at 14.11, and a best of six for 31 against Leyland in early August, Coulthurst helped Whalley to retain the title in 1930. But fitness concerns were now bringing his playing career towards its end. He played only one match for Whalley in 1931, and a single reappearance for East Lancashire, at Haslingden in July 1932, was his unhappy swansong: he pulled a leg muscle in his fifth over, and had to retire from the match and, as it happened, from top-class club cricket, at the age of 38. In all, his fourteen seasons, or part-seasons, in East Lancashire's first eleven had brought him 377 League wickets at 12.81 (and a further 13 in Cup matches), narrowly outscored by his 421 runs at 5.26, with a highest score of 21*.

This was not, however, his highest score in all top cricket. Although he chose not to make himself available for regular three-day cricket after 1919, Coulthurst was not forgotten by the county club. He later recalled that Archie MacLaren told him that he should 'consider yourself selected for the season' for the county's seconds.[66] In fact he did not play in Lancashire II's few matches of 1920. He played in only a single game when they rejoined the Minor Counties competition in 1921, and in only five of their ten games the following year. And no more after that: his relative lack of success at League level meant that his chance for glory at county level, whether seconds or, conceivably, firsts, was now gone, for ever. His bowling figures in his half-dozen second team games were nothing special, 26 wickets at 15.46 with a best of five for 65 against Northumberland in June 1922; but in these six matches he scored more runs, 74, than in any single season of Lancashire League cricket, including an unlikely score of 38 against Durham at Blackpool in August 1922, sharing a partnership of 60 for the last wicket with future England keeper Bill Farrimond.

Blackburn's fastest?

Reporting on Coulthurst's season so far in mid-July 1919, 'Nomad' in the *Blackburn Times* described his successful bowling style like this:

> Lately he has touched the highest plane of his craft. Instead of sending deliveries down of the same pace and flight, without any variation, in the hope that the batsmen will get themselves out, he has concentrated himself to get the opposition dismissed by the use of his wits, and he has developed a slow ball which swings and breaks a lot from the off. This on many occasions has had the desired effect. The secret of his success, however, is good length, and maintaining a terrific pace, which have made him a most deadly bowler.

A few more snippets will help to improve our mental picture of Coulthurst in his heyday.[67] He gripped the ball with his fingers along the seam,

---

66 In an article 'An old demon bowler looks back' in the *Blackburn Times*, 4 August 1967.

67 The descriptions and quotations in the following two paragraphs are taken from articles in the *Blackburn Times* of 12 July 1919 and 4 August 1967; the *Manchester Guardian* of 29 June 1922; and the *Lancashire Evening Telegraph* of 8 January 1970.

using his wrist to move the ball off the pitch when conditions were right, and varied his flight as well as his pace. At League level, at least, these skills, together with his great accuracy, brought him a high proportion of 'bowled' dismissals: 65 of his 101 League victims in 1919 were out bowled, and a further seven were lbw. Against Haslingden in June 1919 – many of his finest performances seem to have been against Haslingden – he bowled six batsmen in an innings with a seventh lbw, and he secured four bowled dismissals in an innings on seven other occasions that season. He was also a disciplined bowler, and claimed never to have been no-balled in his life.

Most reports suggest that his pace was seriously quick: 'His terrific pace proved deadly' ... '[He] bowls fast left, comes from a great height, and can make the ball bounce on any wicket with life in it' ... 'I can picture even now that erect, bespectacled left-hander with the leap as he delivered,[68] and the hurtling speed' ... 'Jos Coulthurst was fast by any standards, and he is still proud of it. He recalls that Neville Cardus once wrote that he was one of the fastest left-arm bowlers of the day – this at the time of Nobby Clark and Bill Voce. And in Harold Larwood's early days he once told Jos, "There's very little in it between McDonald, you and me"' ... 'A genuine fast bowler, he had a distinctive action with a kangaroo leap at the end of a very long run'. He also had a habit of plucking at his left trouser leg before going into his delivery, leaving his flannels thin on his left knee.

ACS sources, however, describe him as only 'fast-medium'. On the basis of the above extracts, that would seem to understate his pace. And yet it has to be reported that two of his wickets for Lancashire II in 1922 were 'stumped' dismissals, by two different wicketkeepers in different matches. If they could stand up to him, maybe he wasn't quite so fast after all?

Outside cricket

Coulthurst's reluctance to make cricket his career arose because of his commitment to a different life. Even before the First World War he had become involved with the Blackburn branch of the Manchester Unity of Oddfellows, a mutual organisation set up to protect and care for its members in the days before the welfare state. He was the secretary of its Blackburn district for many years, and received an inscribed silver cigar case 'as a mark of esteem' from the Darwen branch in 1934.[69] Later he became, in the words of his newspaper interview in 1967, 'a Ministry official', the ambiguity of which phrase it has not been possible to resolve. Was this a post within the Oddfellows organisation, or a civil service appointment?

He was a family man. Jos Coulthurst married Jeanette Watt Forrest in 1927, and they had a daughter, also Jeanette, in 1933. Later, the family's notice of his death described him as a 'very devoted husband and dear father', and there seems no reason to doubt that he benefited from a happy and loving homelife throughout his almost 43 years of marriage.

---

68   This 'leap' no doubt explains how a bowler only 5ft 7½in tall could deliver 'from a great height'.

69   The cigar case was auctioned in Cumbria in November 2007, with an estimated price of £80 to £120.

Cricket was not Jos Coulthurst's only sport. As a schoolboy he was a promising goalkeeper, playing for the Blackburn Schoolboys team that reached the final of the Lancashire Division of the English Schools' Shield competition in 1908, when he was only 14 years old, and presumably not yet at his full, not very substantial, adult height. Sadly, his poor eyesight prevented him taking this game further. Four years later, and again two years after that, Blackburn Rovers were to win the Football League championship; maybe a better-sighted Coulthurst might have had a chance of lasting glory in this other sporting field?

After retiring from cricket he, like many others, took up bowls, and became 'almost as venerated a figure at the Meadows in this game [as at cricket]'.

Josiah Coulthurst was a Blackburn man through and through. He was born there; baptised there; married there to a Blackburn-raised girl; played almost all his cricket there despite being offered the opportunity on occasion to play elsewhere; and lived there for almost his entire life. He finally left his home town when he moved to the coast at Lytham St Annes in the later 1960s, but he was only there a year or two before dying in a geriatric hospital at Wesham, between Blackpool and Preston, on 6 January 1970, at the age of 76. He was buried at Mellor, just to the north of his home town.

Josiah Coulthurst in later life.

But he was also a cricket man through and through, justly proud of his achievements. A photograph accompanying his *Blackburn Times* interview in 1967, when at the age of 73 he was described as bronzed and fit as a fiddle, shows him surrounded by the proud mementoes of a life in cricket. These included his Minor Counties cap; the mounted ball with which he took his 100th wicket in 1919; a clock presented to him by the East Lancashire club; and the championship medals he won with East Lancashire and with Whalley. The accompanying report also says that 'it [was] only recently that he threw away a bundle of old cricket stumps he had broken in two in matches.' He maintained his interest in the East Lancashire club throughout his life, watching them regularly at Alexandra Meadows until his final years.

His failure – if that is the right word – to have a longer first-class career than just his two rainy days at Old Trafford in August 1919 can be put down to various things. Primarily, these were a combination of his own choice of lifestyle, and a falling off in his form after his *annus mirabilis* of 1919. His selection for that one game was no fluke, and neither was it a case of the county giving a token end-of-season appearance to a promising youngster; he was, in any case, already nearer 26 than 25. He had earned it by his performances through the season, and on these performances he might perhaps have been given his county chance a little earlier in the year.

But if he had been, he would not hold the unique distinction that he does: that of being the only cricketer ever to be credited with an appearance in the County Championship without ever setting foot on the field of play.

The absent uncle

What of the other two English instances from the start of this chapter? Let's take **Percy Herbert** first. He was an uncle of Percy Fender, and it was through his nephew's offices that Herbert became a first-class cricketer, in most unusual circumstances. In his biography of Fender, Richard Streeton describes how, on Saturday, 3 July 1920, the Gentlemen of the South played the first day of a first-class match against the Players of the South at The Oval with only ten men, plus a fielding substitute. The professionals scored 551 for nine in the day's play. Over the weekend Fender asked his uncle Percy, 'a good club cricketer', to make up the Gentlemen's eleven. And so:

> on the Monday Percy Herbert travelled to The Oval to play. It rained, however, all day, and again on the Tuesday. There have been instances of cricketers neither batting nor bowling in their solitary first-class match; but to be credited in *Wisden* with playing but never actually seeing a ball bowled, or even treading on the field, must be unique.[70]

As we have seen, not quite unique as far as treading on the field is concerned; but possibly so on the point of not seeing a ball bowled. We'll explore that shortly. But either way, Herbert's record is certainly remarkable.

He was the son of Joseph Herbert, who was Gloucestershire-born but became an important name in cricket in Sussex. In 1870 Joseph was a co-founder of the Brighton Brunswick club, a midweek side with strong associations with the Sussex county side, which drew its players from all the leading clubs of the county. Percy, born in Shoreham in August 1878, is found early in the twentieth century playing as an allrounder for Brighton St James, for Hove, and in 1909, for the first time, for Brighton Brunswick. 'A good club cricketer' seems to be a fair description: local newspapers over the years record him scoring good, but not copious, runs – his only century for the Brunswick came in his debut season for them – and taking good wickets; and also, occasionally, playing alongside his soon-to-be-famous nephew.[71]

After the First World War Herbert seems to have played a little less frequently, but no less successfully. In 1919 he scored only 67 runs for the Brunswick, but also took 11 wickets, including five for 54 against Hastings. In the following season, the earliest date when I can find him playing was 24 June. A week later he scored 58* in a game for Hove, and on Saturday 3 July he scored one and took five wickets over two innings for

---

70   Richard Streeton, *P.G.H.Fender: A Biography*, Faber and Faber, 1981.
71   He was also secretary of the Brunswick club from 1913 to 1920, and club captain, a role probably akin to that of captain of a golf club, from 1921 to 1923.

Hove in an away fixture against Lewes Priory. Later in the season he scored 59 and took six wickets in the same game for Brighton Brunswick against Eastbourne, six for 74 for the Brunswick against Worthing, and seven for 23 for Hove against Old Yorkonians. Good performances, but nothing that suggests that this 42-year-old, as he became in August 1920, should have been playing at a higher level.[72]

And yet, on 3 July of that year that is precisely what he did – officially at least. For that date, as well as being the day of Hove's fixture at the Dripping Pan ground in Lewes, was also the first day of Herbert's one and only first-class match. So although neither he nor anyone else knew it at the time, on that day he was officially playing in two matches, one of them first-class, simultaneously.

There were a number of last-minute drop-outs from the Gentlemen's side for the game at The Oval, including Ranji who, it had been hoped, would captain the side. With Hampshire, Sussex and Kent all playing Championship matches, the opportunity to fill the gaps with gentlemen from 'the South' was very limited, and the ten-man side that took the field when the Players batted was not a strong one. You might have thought that, having won the toss, the Players would have had the decency to insert their depleted opponents; but there was a big crowd in attendance on the first day, who were no doubt keener to see Jack Hobbs and Co bat, rather than a side that – Percy Fender, Jack Crawford and Nigel Haig apart – had only 50 first-class appearances between them. In the event, the Players ran up their big first-day total without taking the game too seriously; a highlight reported in *The Times* was the dismissal, lbw, of Hobbs to 'an atrocious ball ... one of the worst balls bowled at The Oval for many a long day'.[73] Hobbs had, however, made 115 by this time, so the crowd were not too disappointed.[74]

As an allrounder, Herbert would probably have expected to both bat and bowl on days two and three of his first-class debut, if only he had had the chance. We know he batted right-handed – he and his older brother Sidney required their nephew Percy Fender to bat right-handed even though his natural inclination was to bat left. At club level Uncle Percy usually batted in the lower middle order, or less often, at least by 1920, as an opener. We know less of his bowling, though one report of a club game in that year talks of his 'deceptive changing pace', which unfortunately says nothing about whether his basic pace was quick or slow.

His greatest contribution to cricket came, however, not in having a decidedly odd first-class career, but in the nurturing, with brother Sidney, of the oldest son of his sister Lily. She had married Percy Robert Fender in 1891, and Percy George Herbert Fender arrived in August of the following

---

72   All details of his club performances over the years are taken from relevant editions of the *Brighton Gazette.*

73   The bowler was Keith Wilson, of Brighton Brunswick and Sussex. But maybe this was all part of a cunning plan on his part: the source cited in footnote 75 tells us that 'many a wicket he took with what the batsman thought was an easy delivery to hit, and then found out his mistake'.

74   *Wisden*, though, sternly described the match as 'little better than a farce'.

year. Lily was the initial force behind PGH's passion for the game, and remained his most loyal supporter and concerned critic; but it was Uncles Sidney and Percy who instructed him in the basics:

> It was all thanks to my grandfather, Joseph Herbert ... and to my two uncles that I learned to love the game. Whenever I could persuade them to do so we used to play in the [narrow] back garden of 'Melrose' with a tennis ball and a tree stump as a wicket. They batted first with a very old bat but, as I was too young for that, I had to use a tennis racquet and 'first bounce' or 'over the wall' was out. Of course, whenever we broke a window, as sometimes happened, 'the old man' used to get in a temper and that was the end of the game for that day.
>
> With a tennis ball and a tennis racquet for me, and first bounce out, and two agile young men fielding at silly point and silly mid-on, I soon learned to hit the ball where there was no fielder, and that instinct stood me in very good stead all through my cricket life.[75]

The once 'agile young' Percy Herbert was still playing in a good class of club cricket in Hove at least until his late forties. Of his life outside cricket, I regret that I have been able to discover little. The 1911 census records him employed as a 'medical and electrical masseur', whatever that might have involved; but how he earned his crusts in later life, if indeed he had to earn a crust at all - the family was not badly off - I do not know. Late in 1919 he married Dora Breach at Steyning, near Brighton. There were several players called Breach in the Steyning cricket team before the war, and it seems fair to assume that he met his wife through cricket. The marriage, which was childless, lasted 27 years until Dora's death in October 1946, and Percy lived on as a widower for another 11 years. A Hove resident virtually all his life, he died there on 24 January 1958 at the age of 79, and was laid to rest with his wife in Hove Cemetery.

The tomb of the unseen cricketer. Percy Herbert's grave in Hove Cemetery, photographed in 2010.

---

75   From a reminiscence by P.G.H.Fender in the booklet *Brighton Brunswick Club: Centenary Year 1870-1970.* In Streeton's version of the same story, the ball had become a soft rubber ball: you pays your money ... .

The absent second cousin, once removed

We have seen that, despite Richard Streeton's speculation, Percy Herbert was not the only first-class cricketer who never took the field. And there is at least one other candidate for Streeton's other claim for Herbert's uniqueness, too. For Percy Herbert may not be the only first-class cricketer who was not in attendance for any of the play in his only first-class match. **Thomas John Hearne** may have matched him on this; he certainly came close.

One of the extended cricketing family that included J.T. ('Old Jack'), J.W. ('Young Jack'), Frank and Alec Hearne, among many others, T.J.Hearne's life is summarised in the clan history written by a more recent J.W. Hearne,[76] and I don't propose to repeat that summary here. But the circumstances of his non-appearance in first-class cricket bear repetition.

From Monday to Wednesday, 20, 21 and 22 July 1908, Middlesex were due to play the touring Philadelphians in a first-class match at Lord's. The selected side included a number of their Championship regulars, among them Frank Tarrant, Albert Trott and J.T.Hearne; but other regulars such as Pelham Warner and B.J.T.Bosanquet were rested while other less experienced players were given a game. At the last minute, J.T.Hearne had to withdraw, and his second cousin once removed, T.J.Hearne, was sent for at short notice to take his place. The game began in dull weather on the Monday, and proceeded apace. Tarrant and Trott, bowling unchanged (as they did throughout the match), dismissed the visitors for 58, whereupon the ten batsmen of Middlesex fell for 92, with four taken by Bart King and two by 'Ranji' Hordern. The Philadelphians only managed 55 in their second effort, and Middlesex knocked off the runs needed for victory for the loss of three more wickets. All this on the first day.

In Middlesex's first innings, T.J.Hearne is listed as 'absent', for he had not arrived in time to bat. *The Sportsman* confirms that he never took the field in the entire match: '[Hearne] made his first appearance in first-class cricket without having stepped out of the players' pavilion',[77] but it appears that he may have arrived before the game ended,[78] though his time of arrival at Lord's is not recorded. It may have been during his side's brief (six-over) second innings; it may even have been towards the end of the Philadelphians' second innings, when it was decided that he need not rush to get ready to field as the visitors were collapsing quite happily without him. In either of those cases, he would at least have seen play in action. But if, as is entirely possible, he did not arrive until after Middlesex had secured the victory, then he would have joined Percy Herbert in not witnessing any play in the match that constituted his entire first-class career. Sadly, it is unlikely that we will ever find out for sure.

The question also arises: what were the circumstances that brought about T.J.'s brush with fame? Why did J.T.Hearne drop out of the Philadelphia

---

76   J.W 'Jack' Hearne, *Wheelwrights to Wickets*, Boundary Books, 1996.

77   *The Sportsman*, 21 July 1908

78   The ACS book of *First-Class Matches 1908* tells us that 'he would have batted in the second innings had it been necessary'.

game at a late stage, to give his distant cousin his chance for glory?

The answer is that it was not injury that kept J.T. out of the Philadelphians match: goodness knows how much shorter it might have been if he had been able to play. In fact, his father William Hearne had died on 17 July, two days after celebrating his 80th birthday; and it was surely this that rendered J.T. unavailable to play at Lord's on 20 July.[79] How it came about that J.T.'s absence from the Philadelphia game was not known until the last minute; and why, when they found this out, Middlesex chose to call up a player who was unable to be at the ground for most of the scheduled first day when surely there were other no less unsuitable amateurs closer at hand, are further mysteries that are unlikely to be resolved.

As a cricketer, Thomas John Hearne was principally a left-arm bowler: slow left-arm according to *Wheelwrights to Wickets*, medium-pace according to the *Who's Who of Cricketers*. It is implied in *Wheelwrights* that he was a stock bowler for Berkshire for three years in his teens, but this is not borne out by other available sources: certainly he played no Minor Counties cricket for them at this time. He played the occasional game for Middlesex II between 1906 and 1909. These were, however, not Minor Counties Championship matches: Middlesex Seconds did not join that competition until 1935.

His only experience of Minor Counties Championship cricket therefore came in eight games for Berkshire in 1922 and 1923. He began well, taking nine wickets in his first match, with six for 44 and three for 40 against Cornwall at Reading, but could not as much as double this tally in his remaining seven matches.

The Berkshire side of 1923, with Thomas Hearne, now 36, standing at the left hand end of the back row. Percy Chapman is seated second from the left. H.M.Hinde, who appears elsewhere in this book, is standing fourth from the left.

---

79 In other circumstances, J.T.'s older brother William, who played a couple of Second XI matches for Middlesex in 1907 and 1908, might have seemed a more natural replacement from within the Hearne family. But he, of course, was ruled out for the same reason as J.T.

T.J.Hearne spent his later years as a groundsman and cricket coach at Bryanston School, but died six weeks before he would have turned 60. His death was unrecorded in *Wisden* at the time; but his unusual first-class career finally earned him the distinction of a Wisden obituary 47 years later, in the serendipitous 'Supplementary Obituaries' published in 1994.

Two more Englishmen

Although Jos Coulthurst, Percy Herbert and T.J.Hearne are the only cricketers to 'appear but not appear' in their only first-class matches in England, one and quite probably two of the others 'never seen', as named in the list at the start of this chapter, are English by birth.

Little is known about the background, or even the name, of **W.Hunt,** who earned his claim to fame in a two-day match at Nicetown in Philadelphia that started on Independence Day in 1882. Efforts to find out more have unfortunately fallen on stony ground. Only 47.1 four-ball overs were possible in this game because of rain, in which time Hunt never made it to the crease. He played a few other club games in Philadelphia around this time, without doing anything remarkable. He seems to have been mainly a batsman rather than a bowler, but beyond that I cannot go. In his first-class match he was representing 'English Residents' against 'American Born', so presumably he was of English birth. About 3,000 boys christened Walter or William Hunt, with or without middle names, were registered in England and Wales between 1845 and 1865, the most likely period for the birth of 'our' W.Hunt. Identifying which one was the cricketer is a task too far for the present book. Or maybe he was a Wilfred, or a Wilbur, or even a Wayne, or ...

Hemish Ilangaratne going out to bat for Hemel Hempstead in July 2011.

If Hunt's birthplace was probably in England, that of **Hemish Ilangaratne** certainly was. He was born in Derby on 25 July 1987 and has played club and county cricket in Hertfordshire for several years, including county age-group cricket since the age of 12. A stylish right-handed batsman, usually an opener, and very occasional right-arm medium-pace bowler, he has represented Hemel Hempstead regularly in the Home Counties Premier League since his first game in 2003, when he was still only 15 years old: in 2011 he was the club's first-team captain. He has also appeared occasionally for Hertfordshire in the Minor Counties Championship.

His surname indicates a Sri Lankan family origin, and in the records in CricketArchive he has featured in just one match, of any description, in that country. This was his one and only first-class match, in which he turned out for Kurunegala Youth CC against Singha SC in the Welagedara Stadium at Kurunegala in a Premier Championship match in November 2006. On the first day only 39.2 overs were possible, in which Ilangaratne's side reached 102 for three; rain then prevented play on either of the other two scheduled days. In the CA scorecard he is listed to bat at an unlikely number 10, but wherever he was due to come in, sadly he never got the chance to do so; and for whatever reason he was not included in the Kurunegala Youth side for any of their remaining games of the season, nor subsequently.

The unluckiest of them all

You might have thought that those already listed as 'never seen' were the unluckiest cricketers of them all. But at least they are bona fide first-class cricketers, because the game in which they were due to play did at least get started. So spare a thought for those even less fortunate players who were selected to play in a first-class match, but never did so because conditions prevented the game ever starting. 'Match abandoned without a ball bowled' means that, in statistical terms, it was not a match at all – and so those selected are not credited with a first-class appearance. If this was the only first-class match for which they were selected, it means they were forever denied the kudos of being able to call themselves a first-class cricketer; so near, yet so far.

Teams have not always been announced for abandoned matches, and so I cannot provide a full list of these unfortunates. From a trawl of *Wisden*, of Ray Webster's *First-class Cricket in Australia*, and of some other sources, I have identified 18 of them; no doubt there are others in other countries. Here are the details of the unlucky 18, and the matches they were due to play in; very brief biographical information is given where known:

- N.Morice, MCC v Yorkshire, Scarborough, 1891. There was no play on the first day of matches on the same dates in London and Nottingham, though both were able to progress on their second and third days; but play in Scarborough was ruled out altogether. Norman Morice was an Old Malvernian – he captained the school's side in 1882 – who generally opened the batting, as well as taking a few wickets, in the matches recorded for him in the Cricket-Archive database.

- A.J.Woodward, Warwickshire v Leicestershire, Coventry, 1908. Woodward is referred to by Robert Brooke in his book on F.R.Foster[80] as a 'local amateur'. Simultaneous matches at nearby Worcester and Northampton were able to get started on their second days, but Coventry was unplayable throughout.

- G.Parnell and A.C.Yates, New South Wales v Queensland, Sydney, 1921/22, and W.M.Forbes for Queensland in the same match. This was a friendly match from the days before Queensland were

80   Robert Brooke, *F.R.Foster: The Fields Were Sudden Bare*, ACS Publications, 2011.

admitted to the Sheffield Shield competition. Yates appears to have been primarily a bowler; nothing is known, by the writer or by CricketArchive, of the other two.

- Captain J.L.Quinn, Essex v Surrey, The Oval, 1924. He was named in the Essex twelve for this game, so might have been omitted from the final eleven in any case.

- S.G.Wills, Gloucestershire v Kent, Bristol, 1927. There's a bit of a mystery here. Wills is listed in the Gloucestershire eleven in *Wisden*, but he was not in the twelve for the same game as printed in *The Times*. It may be *Wisden* that is in error: they also included an otherwise-unknown 'J.S.Valentine' in the Kent side, but the probability is that this was an error for B.H.Valentine, who was in his first season for Kent.

- G.Bishop, Northamptonshire v Yorkshire, Harrogate, 1930. Listed as 'C.Bishop' in *Wisden*, but local newspapers in Northampton confirm that his first name was George. He had been twelfth man for the match against Glamorgan at Peterborough on 19 to 22 July, and was promoted to the first team for the following game at Harrogate, replacing the injured Reg Partridge. Dreadful weather in Yorkshire ruled out any chance of play and Bishop was passed over for subsequent games, even though Partridge did not return until mid-August. Bishop, who may or may not have been the same cricketer as the G.A.Bishop who played a few matches for Leicestershire II in 1931, was educated at St John's School at Tiffield, near Brackley – also the *alma mater* of Fred Bakewell – but attempts to find out more about him have been thwarted by the fact that St John's was a reformatory school, whose records for the period are not yet open to the public.

- A.W.Flugge, A.G.Harding, J.C.A.Pizzey, A.H.F.Rofe and H.N.M.Yeates. All five players were listed in the Victoria twelve for the Sheffield Shield match against Queensland at Brisbane in 1930/31, so at least four of them would have become first-class cricketers had the game started. Victoria were fielding, or intending to field, an under-strength side, because the Brisbane game was due to take place simultaneously with a match at Melbourne between Victoria and the visiting West Indian tourists. The relatively unimpressive performances in other matches of Jack Pizzey, Arthur Rofe and Herbert Yeates, as recorded in CricketArchive, do not allow us to deduce which were primarily batsmen, and which bowlers. The other two do not even get as far as an entry in the CA database.

- N.V.Butler, L.E.Liddell, G.A.Marlow and S.J.Norcup, Minor Counties v Warwickshire, Birmingham, 1954. All four were long-serving Minor Counties players who deserved their expected first-class appearances, but it was not to be. Norman Butler (Buckinghamshire, 1950-1968) was a batsman who bowled a bit; Larry Liddell (Northumberland, 1947-1958) a hard-hitting batsman, who captained the Minor Counties in a non-first-class (and rain-ruined) match against the touring New Zealanders in 1958; Geoff Marlow (Lincolnshire, 1946-1957) a bowling all-rounder who also played football for Lincoln City: a winger, he scored 26 goals for them in 80 league appearances between 1937/38 and 1948/49; and Samuel Norcup (Staffordshire, 1946-1958) an opening bowler.

- D.Urquhart, Queensland v Victoria, Brisbane, 1970/71. Like Quinn (above), Donald Urquhart was named in a twelve for this game, so might not have made the final cut. He was a specialist batsman, who was once run out for 99 playing for Queensland Colts against NSW Colts. He also played for a Queensland Country XI against MCC in 1970/71, when he was dismissed caught-and-bowled by Colin Cowdrey: not perhaps the most auspicious ending to an innings.

Chapter Four

Runs Aplenty

Over 300 cricketers have scored a century in their first innings in first-class cricket. Some have gone on to cricketing fame, and perhaps a bit of fortune too.

But eight of them have a special distinction: after scoring a century in their debut innings, for one reason or another they never batted again at first-class level. Their final career averages, if they have one, are therefore superior to Don Bradman's, but their names – still less their lives, in or out of cricket – are known to few.

A century in only first-class innings

N.F.Callaway	207	NSW v Queensland	Sydney	1914/15
S.E.Wootton	105	Victoria v Tasmania	Hobart	1923/24
H.H.E.Grangel	108	Victoria v Tasmania	Melbourne	1935/36
M.N.Harbottle	156	Army v Oxford University	Camberley	1938
S.Harding	100*	Sinhalese v Burgher	Colombo	1988/89
K.Seth	125*	Madhya Pradesh v Vidarbha	Indore	2000/01
J.S.D.Moffat	169	Cambridge Univ v Oxford Univ	Oxford	2002
A.S.Sharma	185*	Oxford Univ v Cambridge Univ	Oxford	2010

The latest of the three instances in England – by a New Zealander, incidentally – is so recent that the player concerned may disqualify himself from the list in the future.[81] The other two British-based players have something else in common: both achieved greater fame in fields other than cricket. It is around these other fields that we must focus our explorations of their lives.

Keeping the peace

Michael Neale Harbottle is most renowned not for his day of cricketing glory, nor for his fine record in the Army, but for what he did after retiring from his Army career. It is on the strength above all of those later activities that he is the only cricketer in this book to have earned an entry in the *Dictionary of National Biography*, which encapsulates him as 'army officer and peace campaigner'. It was the second of those facets that brought him a degree of fame, not to say notoriety, in the later part of his life.

Born into a military family at Littlehampton on 7 February 1917, Harbottle was expected to follow his father into the Navy, but bunions meant that

---

81   Avinash Sharma has now returned to New Zealand. A doctor, his opportunities
      to play further first-class cricket may be limited.

he fell foul of the Navy selection panel. The Army, however, weren't so choosy. As his obituary in *The Guardian* tells us, 'The army, ignoring his feet, cheerfully accepted him into Sandhurst, where he captained the cricket team ... .'

And that, and a similar reference in *The Times*, is the only reference to cricket in any of his broadsheet obituaries, or in his *DNB* entry.

Harbottle went on to a distinguished, if slightly abbreviated, Army career. He entered Sandhurst from Marlborough College in 1935, and was commissioned into the Oxfordshire and Buckinghamshire Light Infantry on leaving Sandhurst in 1937. Promoted to lieutenant in 1940 and captain in 1945, his war service was principally in Italy. He was mentioned in dispatches in 1945 for his 'gallant and distinguished services' in that country, and during the war he lost two fingers on his right hand.[82] (He was, perhaps fortunately, a left-hander.) Army service continued through the 1950s, with promotions to Major in 1950 and Lt-Colonel in 1959, and in the latter year he was awarded the OBE in the Birthday Honours List. Also in 1959 he became Commander of the 1st Battalion of the Royal Green Jackets, a post he held until 1962. In that year, as well as being promoted to Colonel, he also took on his most prominent overseas role since the war, as garrison commander of the British forces in Aden, then emerging as a highly sensitive anti-colonial flashpoint.

He held this post for two years, and then returned to the UK for two years before – by now a Brigadier – moving to what was to prove a life-changing posting as Chief of Staff of the United Nations peacekeeping force in another trouble-spot, Cyprus. Here he developed a role for peacekeeping that differed from the more usual role of pacification: as he interpreted it, military peacekeeping involved mediation and conciliation, and not – or not just – intervening actively to curb aggression between two opposing forces. Under this view, the UN forces were to use their weapons only in self-defence.

So successful was Harbottle in this role that, when his period of duty ended in 1968, the UN's Secretary-General, U Thant,[83] wanted it to be extended. But his belief that it was a self-evident truth 'that peacekeeping and peace-building were indispensable and invaluable instruments of peace', and that 'there was more to soldiering than fighting or preparing to fight'[84] went down badly at the Ministry of Defence, and the Secretary-General's request was declined. Whereupon, at the age of 51, Brigadier Harbottle retired from the Army.

There followed a brief period as chief security officer on behalf of a mining company in Sierra Leone, which ended when, late in 1969, he was expelled from the country after being robbed of £1.5m-worth of diamonds by armed bandits at the airport in Freetown. As his *DNB* entry says, his

---

82   Some sources say three. His obituary in *The Times* on 7 May 1997 contented itself with 'several'.

83   There is a photograph of Harbottle with U Thant in *The Times* of 16 June 1970.

84   Words taken from his obituary in *The Independent*, 14 May 1997.

expulsion was based 'on the implausible pretext that the company had set up its own hijack'.

The 1970s saw him developing his views on peacekeeping, writing a number of well-received books on the subject, and in 1978 collating the *Peacekeeper's handbook*, which became a standard instruction manual for UN forces acting in this role.

So far, so not particularly shocking. But the *DNB* tells us that 'during the 1980s [his] work took a disconcerting turn'. Well, that rather depends on your point of view. From peacekeeping in the relatively small scale of individual conflicts, Harbottle's thinking moved to a more global scale, leading him to the conclusion that 'international confidence-building would only work through disarmament'.[85] At this particular point in the Cold War, such a view was seen as heresy, especially coming from a former career soldier; but it was one that would shape the rest of Harbottle's life.

Between the early 1970s and his death in 1997, Harbottle was, at one time or another, a leading member of, or consultant to, over half a dozen organisations whose objective was the furtherance of peace. These included the International Peace Academy (1971-1973), the World Disarmament Campaign (1980-1982), and the organisation with which he is perhaps most associated, the International Generals for Peace and Disarmament (1981-1990) and its post-Cold War successor, the Worldwide Consultative Association of Retired Generals and Admirals.[86] In 1981 he and his strongly like-minded second wife Eirwen co-founded the youth organisation Peace Child International, and two years later they founded the Centre for International Peacebuilding, of which he remained a director until his death.

In the 1980s it was inevitable that such organisations sought discussions with counterparts in Eastern Europe. In some of the corridors of power this led to Harbottle and his fellows being branded as Marxists and traitors – labels that stuck to him, in some quarters at least, for the rest of his life.[87] However, as his obituarists wrote in *The Independent*, 'No-one who really knew Harbottle thought he was in any way politicised'; and 'Like many basically good men [he] was a little naïf about the company he kept, but there is no doubt that his heart lay with the peacemakers. Real soldiers love peace, because they've seen the obscenity of war and heard the ranting of so-called patriots too often'.[88] In his strivings for peace, Michael Harbottle was simply an honest and disinterested idealist.

Cricketing glory

So, not just an obscure cricketer, then. But a cricketer nonetheless ... .

Harbottle showed his abilities at the game early. As a 14-year-old in 1931

---

85   *The Independent*, 14 May 1997.

86   A fuller list of the organisations in which he participated can be found in his entry in *Who Was Who*.

87   This may be the reason why there is no obituary of him in the newspaper that routinely prints obituaries of lesser-known senior military figures, the *Daily Telegraph*.

88   From a letter from Michael Hawthorne printed in *The Guardian* on 28 May 1997, following up the paper's initial obituary on 9 May.

he played at Lord's in the annual Under-16s match between a Lord's XI and C.F.Tufnell's XI, batting for the Lord's XI alongside his brother John.[89] He captained the Lord's XI in the same fixture in 1932, and then spent his last three school years in the Marlborough eleven, where however he did not set the world alight. From the figures in *Wisden* his dogged left-handed batting in the school's middle order brought him just 753 runs over the seasons 1933 to 1935, with a highest score of 72 against Harrow in 1934.

He was at Sandhurst for the 1936 and 1937 seasons, and also in 1936 he began his long, if intermittent, association with the Dorset Minor Counties side. Playing under a residential qualification – the family home was at Wareham – and now opening the batting, he appeared in thirteen Minor Counties Championship matches for Dorset between 1936 and 1938, scoring 83 against Cornwall in his third innings for the county, and 96 against Wiltshire in 1937.

The Sandhurst side of 1937.
Standing (l to r): J.North, B.E.W.Henson (wk), S.I.Howard-Jones, J.M.Hutton,
A.F.Campbell, A.G.Roberts, J.Weston, J.Clark.
Seated: D.R.Dalglish, G.A.F.Steede, Capt J.P.A.Graham, M.N.Harbottle,
A.M.Champion, J.W.Hodges.

By 1938 the Army's only remaining first-class fixtures were their games against the two Universities, their matches against the other Services and the overseas tourists having been downgraded to two-day games earlier in the decade.

Despite his successes in the Minor Counties competition and for various Sandhurst-based military sides, Harbottle was not selected for the match against Cambridge University at Fenner's in May. But representative Army

---

89   Harbottle's two siblings, older brothers Anthony and John, were both killed in the Second World War.

sides, then as now, inevitably showed many comings and goings from one match to the next. So it was no great surprise that the Army made four changes for the game against Oxford to be played at the Royal Military College at Camberley,[90] due to begin on Saturday 25 June. One of these saw Harbottle selected in place of opener Lancelot Grove, who had made a century at Cambridge.

The match began, on a warm but fresh day, with Harbottle opening the Army's innings just as, 30 miles away at Lord's, Wally Hammond was completing an innings of 240 against Australia in the Second Test. The Army lost their first two wickets for 56, but then Harbottle was joined by Reginald Hudson, who had also not played at Cambridge, and who was playing in what turned out to be the last of his 27 first-class matches. Between them they added 276 for the third wicket,[91] against a limited bowling attack containing no big names. The more experienced man dominated the stand, Hudson scoring all round the wicket in making his 147 in 190 minutes, which included a five and 22 fours. Harbottle is reported as giving chances when 23 and 71 – we do not know how straightforward, or otherwise, these might have been – but that apart, the partnership looked impregnable throughout.

The two partners were eventually out in quick succession – it is not clear from available reports who was dismissed first, though it was probably Hudson.[92] Harbottle eventually fell for 156, caught at the wicket off the occasional slow left-armers of Desmond Eagar. His innings was described as 'stylish' by the *Manchester Guardian*; from *The Times* we learn that he scored most of his runs on the off side, and that 'he showed sound defence for four and a quarter hours'. The *Daily Telegraph* preferred to call it 'stout defence'. Either way it was an effective, rather than a scintillating, innings, especially by comparison with Hudson's. But it was a century on debut and at the time, the fourth-highest debut innings in all first-class cricket in England;[93] and not a bad first day in first-class cricket.[94]

The Army ran up 450 for nine in 107 overs on that first day, and declared at this score when rain severely delayed the start on the following Monday. The University were then bowled out for 129, and were 174 for three in

---

90   Although the venue for this match is always identified as 'Camberley', which is in Surrey, the ground itself was and still is located in Berkshire.

91   This is the highest two-man partnership ever shared in by a batsman playing his only first-class innings, though K.Seth [see earlier table] also batted in a partnership of 276, in his case unbroken, but with two different partners (one retired hurt after adding 249). Incidentally, Seth is unique among those scoring a century in his only first-class innings, in that throughout his on-field career as a first-class batsman he did not witness a single wicket falling.

92   Available reports of Harbottle's innings are limited to the brief reports in the national papers. Strangely, the local *Camberley News*, though reporting regularly on matches at the RMC, makes no mention whatsoever of Harbottle's match.

93   Behind scores of 227 by Tom Marsden (Sheffield and Leicester) in 1826; 195* by James Ricketts (Lancashire) in 1867; and 158* by John Human (Cambridge University) in 1932.

94   To date, among cricketers making their debuts in England, only Hubert Doggart, with 215 for Cambridge University in 1948, and Mike Powell, with 200* for Glamorgan in 1997, have bettered Harbottle's tally of 156 runs on his first day as a first-class cricketer.

the follow-on when the game finished on Tuesday. Thus Harbottle had no second chance to bat; he also made no catches, and his even-more-occasional-than-Eagar's slow left-armers were not given an outing. So he had to be content with just an innings of 156 to mark his first-class debut; and who wouldn't be?

This was Harbottle's first century in any of the matches whose scores I have traced, but he wasted no time in getting his second. On 22 July he made 109 for the Army against the Royal Navy at Lord's, all before lunch on the first day of a two-day fixture. *The Times* described this innings as 'most enjoyable' and 'a splendid all-round display', but also 'workmanlike', a comment which seems a little harsh for a pre-lunch century. Described this time as 'an engaging left-hander', he is reported as making good use of the pull-stroke, to give the lie to any suggestions of him being solely an off-side player. He enjoyed another good stand with Hudson during this innings, this time of 81.

There were no more first-class fixtures for the Army in 1938; had there been, then on this form Harbottle would surely have been an automatic selection, if available. He did however play for them in one further important match, a two-day game against the Australians at Aldershot in mid-August. On the face of it, his scores of one and 28 were nothing to write home about, but the latter was the top score in the Army's second innings of 119, and their second-highest of the match. A photograph of the teams in this match shows him, tall, relaxed and cravatted, alongside Lindsay Hassett. But then, most cricketers would look tall alongside Lindsay Hassett.

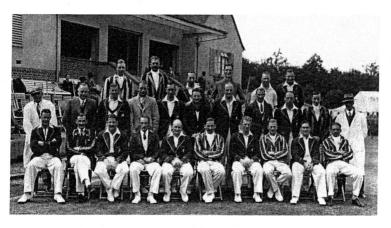

Teams in the Army v Australians two-day match at Aldershot in August 1938. Harbottle is fourth from left in the back row. The tourists, sans Bradman, won by an innings. The Australians, with piping on their blazer lapels, are, in the back row (l to r): A.L.Hassett, C.W.Walker (in white shirt), S.G.Barnes; middle row: E.L.McCormick, E.S.White, W.J.O'Reilly, J.H.W.Fingleton; front row: W.A.Brown, L.O'B. Fleetwood-Smith, S.J.McCabe, B.A.Barnett, C.L.Badcock.

He did not play in the Army's only first-class match of 1939, at Cambridge early in June – which proved to be the Army's last-ever first-class fixture as an independent team. Neither did he play for Dorset in that year. Their season started little more than a month before the declaration of war, when no doubt there were more pressing matters for 2nd Lt Harbottle to attend to. He did however play in the Army's one-day game against the West Indians at Lord's in May, when he was bowled for a duck. He was also in the side that started a rain-ruined match against the Navy at Aldershot in July, in which the Army did not get to start their innings.

Then it was off to war, and there is no further record of him playing cricket for 12 years. When the war ended he was named in an article in *The Cricketer* as a player for the future of Army cricket: 'he might yet fill the gap which will be felt when Godfrey Bryan retires from Army cricket,'[95] but whether because of his hand injury, or because military duties took priority, or because his place was indeed blocked by Bryan (who played his last senior match for the Army in 1951), Harbottle did not resume a place in their side until 1952.

In the previous year he had reappeared for Dorset for the first time since 1938, making his only century in Minor Counties cricket in the second innings of his first match – 105 out of 147 against Oxfordshire at Oxford, reaching his century in 2½ hours. According to the *Oxford Mail* he 'used all the left-hander's strokes, his timing on the off side being as near perfection as one could wish'. In the same year he also made 84 and 77 against Berkshire at Reading, and averaged over 50 for the season for the only time in his Minor Counties career. *Wisden* in 1952 commented that 'with [his] return after many years' absence, the [Dorset] batting was considerably strengthened'.

He was to play regularly for Dorset in 1952 and 1953, approaching another century in the latter year when he made 98 against Wiltshire at Swindon. He made one final appearance for the county in 1956, ending his career for them by being run out, just as he had been in his first innings for the county.[96]

By now his appearances for the Army were also less frequent, as the side became dominated by National Servicemen who had already begun to make their mark in the first-class county game. Three matches in 1952 were followed by another lengthy intermission, before in 1958 and 1959 Harbottle, now in his forties, returned to the side as captain. For the Army he could not recapture his pre-war form, his best innings for them after his return in 1952 being a score of 42 against a strong Hampshire side, whose main bowlers were Butch White, Vic Cannings and Mervyn Burden, on the County Ground at Southampton in July 1958.

And so, after a final game against the RAF in August 1959, Lt-Col Harbottle left the active cricketing scene. Other life-defining activities were now to take over.

---

95   E.H.Fitzherbert, The Regular Army and First-Class Cricket, in *The Cricketer* 1945, p 178.

96   These were the only two run-out dismissals of his 42-innings Minor Counties' career.

Envoi

Michael Harbottle was married twice – first to Alison Jane Humfress in 1940, and following a divorce, to Eirwen Simonds (née Jones) in 1972. The first marriage produced a son and a daughter; the son, Simon Neale Harbottle, followed his father into the Army and played for them in a non-first-class match against Oxford University in 1973, bowling out Imran Khan in the University's first innings, and in turn being bowled by Imran for 38, when the Army batted. He also took three of the four wickets that fell in the University's second innings.

Harbottle's newspaper obituaries give a kindly insight into the character of this devoted and sincere campaigner for peace. *The Guardian* called him a 'gentle warrior', though it also mentioned 'a hasty temper'. *The Independent*'s obituary described him as 'mischievous ... [but] with a direct common-sense approach'. A follow-up letter in *The Guardian* tells us more: '[He] really enjoyed life. In particular he enjoyed human beings. He was a good companion who carried over into his work for peace the resourceful and considerate camaraderie that turns a good soldier into a fine leader ... [He] was a good man and a brave one'.[97]

Harbottle died in hospital at Oxford on 30 April 1997, at the age of 80.[98] Cricket was probably not uppermost in the minds of those who subsequently paid tribute to him, nor when the Last Post and Reveille were sounded at his memorial service at St James', Piccadilly in July of that year.

But there is one final cricketing memory that deserves to be recorded here. In *Wisden Cricket Monthly* in December 1984, David Frith reported on a sale of cricketana at Southampton in which the star lot – one that 'enjoyed much exposure on local television and radio' – was the box that Harbottle wore at the crease for 27 years. Reported to be 'the final resting-place of a bee which stung its owner during the 1934 Marlborough v Cheltenham match' [please feel free to wince at this point], it had also provided protection during his 156 at Camberley in 1938, and indeed for the rest of his active cricketing career. It sold for £50, bought by a member of his family who, in Frith's nicely-chosen words, was 'presumably unable to face the future without the family heirloom'.

So, for all his achievements away from the cricket field, Michael Harbottle's family valued him as a cricketer too; one who died with the distinction – still unique – of being the only Englishman to score a century in his one and only first-class innings.

Scotland's full-back

'Cricket was always my first love'. Not words you'd expect to hear from a Scotsman with four caps for his country at rugby. And yet ...

For the only Briton other than Michael Harbottle to score a century in his one and only first-class innings is a friendly, quietly-spoken and modest

---

97   Letter from Professor Adam Curle, printed in *The Guardian*, 9 May 1997.
98   His death certificate confirms 30 April as the date of his death, and not 1 May as given in *Wisden* and some contemporary newspapers.

Scotsman, **Stuart Moffat,** or in full, John Stuart David Moffat. Born in Edinburgh in August 1977 into a cricket- and rugby-playing family, his upward progression in both sports was swift, and he reached national age-group sides in both sports while still at Edinburgh Academy. Rugby began to dominate when he went to study economics at Loughborough University, and while there he enjoyed a period as a semi-professional in English club rugby. A career-threatening injury in April 1999 – he broke both the tibia and fibula of his left leg – put him out of the game for a year, but he returned to rugby during postgraduate studies at Cambridge, playing in the Varsity matches of 2000 and 2001.

Shortly before the end of his two years at Cambridge he signed full-time professional terms with Glasgow Rugby – at the time, one of Scotland's two top professional sides. His brief first-class cricket career followed before he finally left Cambridge in 2002, but so successful was he at Glasgow that by November of that year he was playing the first of his four full rugby internationals for Scotland. Over the years, club rugby took him from Glasgow to The Borders (later Border Reivers), then to France with Castres, back to the Reivers, and finally to Italy with Viadana, before he retired from the professional game after the 2007/08 season.

Now married to Emma, a former England lacrosse international who he met at Loughborough, and looking to find a new career outside sport, he has been able to return to playing cricket for Grange CC in the summer months, but as time moves on he no longer turns out regularly in amateur rugby in the winter.

From that brief narrative, we may draw two themes – two choices – that go to the heart of Stuart's life in cricket, or better, his life in sport. The first concerns the competing claims for his time and affection of cricket and rugby; while the second concerns the competing claims of sport and what, for want of a better word, we may call real life.

Cricket or rugby?

Stuart was a cricketer before he started to make his mark at rugby. His days as a cricketer began, as with so many sons of cricketing families, with summer weekends spent watching older members of the family playing the game. Early progress was rapid. He was in the Edinburgh Academy first eleven at the age of 14, getting his name into *Wisden* for the first time in 1993. By the age of 16 he was batting at No.3 for Scotland's Under-19s against India Under-17s – not a happy start, though, as he was lbw second ball – and within a year he was an automatic choice at that level. In July 1995, still only 17, he made 106 against Wales SCA Under-19s at Abergavenny, and in 1996 he captained the Under-19s, leading from the front with innings of 112* against ESCA Under-19s at Jesmond, and later 79 against England Under-17s at Scarborough. Both scores were made against a bowling attack that included a 17-year-old Graeme Swann, who Stuart today remembers as being, even at that age, 'very very sure of himself'.[99]

---

99   Throughout this section, unattributed quotes from Stuart are taken from my meetings with him on 30 June 2010.

Cricket was Stuart's stronger suit, until he developed the build for rugby: 'I was quite a late bloomer, 16, 17, and all of a sudden I got quite big and realised I was quite good at rugby as well.'[100] He was in the fifteen for his last two years at Edinburgh Academy, during which period he also played for Scottish Schools.[101]

He played both cricket and rugby during a gap year in Sydney, before heading to Loughborough in September 1996. During the three years studying for his BSc, his rugby prowess caught the eye of the ambitious Rotherham Titans club, for whom he played as a semi-professional while still at university. Opportunities for cricket were more limited: after all, there was studying to be done as well, and Stuart was concerned to secure a good degree. With money being dangled before him from the emerging professional rugby scene, 'rugby sort of took over because it was lucrative and the path into professional cricket wasn't as straightforward.' So he played only a handful of cricket matches at Loughborough, not making it into the sides that reached the finals of the BUSA Championships in 1997 and 1998, though he recalls making a score of 167* in a friendly against another university during his time there.

His serious injury in April 1999, playing (to the chagrin of his father back in Edinburgh) for English Universities against Welsh Universities at Cardiff, ended his immediate ambitions in rugby. The medics suggested that his rugby days might be over, so once he was sufficiently mobile he took a year in South Africa 'to resurrect the cricket career, because I had pretty much given up rugby at that stage'. Although playing mostly second-team cricket for Claremont in Constantia, Stuart recalls this as 'a very worthwhile experience', for his more general rehabilitation as well as for his cricket.

Returning from South Africa, he was able to take up the postgraduate place at Cambridge that he had sought before leaving Loughborough. Two years studying economics and management at St Edmund's College followed; and now the choice had to be made: cricket or rugby? 'I had intended to play as much cricket as I could [at Cambridge], because I went in with the theory that if you can bat on Scottish wickets, you can go down south and bat on those wickets quite easily because they play a bit truer down there. But time slipped away from me in the first year. I was working pretty hard academically, and thought that I might struggle in the exams if I didn't dedicate a significant amount of time to that [so I] never got involved [in cricket]. The rugby at Cambridge was fantastic fun but pretty time-consuming and it just kind of took over.'

It did so to such an extent, and with such success, that Stuart played in the Varsity matches of 2000, in his preferred position of full-back, and 2001, on the wing,[102] and in November 2001 he came very close to selection

---

100   'Quite big': Stuart stands 6ft 3in tall, and in his professional days weighed around 15½ stone.

101   It would be remiss of me not to mention Stuart's acknowledged debt to Garry Bowe of Edinburgh Academy, for his sporting development as a student there, and to Jim Love, then the Scotland cricket coach.

102   Cambridge lost both matches.

as full-back for the full Scotland side, against Argentina, while still an amateur. As his MA course came to an end in May 2002, Stuart signed as a full-time professional for Heineken Cup side Glasgow Rugby; a career in the 15-man game beckoned, and cricket would have to take a back seat.

But it had not disappeared from his life altogether. By now, Cambridge University and Anglia Polytechnic University[103] had joined forces as Cambridge UCCE for the majority of their first-class programme, but the senior university was on its own for the annual first-class match against Oxford. Stuart recalls that they were struggling to piece together a solid side, and in the hope of beefing the team up a bit, cricket coach Chris Scott 'pretty much asked around the rugby club to see if they had anyone who could play cricket.' Two players came forward: Stuart, and a New Zealander and fellow rugby Blue, Mark Chapman-Smith. From such chance events does a degree of fame arise.

Stuart now picked up a cricket bat for the first time for a while, and found form immediately, with a score of 89 against the Quidnuncs on 3 June, and innings of 60 and 47 against the Combined Services at Aldershot on 19 to 21 June. The one-day Varsity match against Oxford – still at Lord's, although the four-day game had moved back to the university cities – was due on 25 June, but despite his good form Stuart was not selected: '[Scott] didn't pick me, not because I wasn't playing well but because I'd gone on holiday to Barbados for a week and been to a couple of May Balls, so my preparation wasn't what you'd probably call ideal.'

So he was stuck with twelfth-man duties as Cambridge lost at Lord's. During the game, his fellow late-selection Mark Chapman-Smith scored 32, but also suffered a thigh strain. He would not be fit for the four-day game in The Parks at Oxford starting the following day so, unusual preparations notwithstanding, Stuart was drafted into the side.

What followed was 'a day that I would put up there as my greatest day ... it would go down as my proudest memory.' It was one of those days when everything just conspired favourably. Coming in at 220 for four on a pitch that he recalls as 'very dry, very flat, and with a very quick outfield', for Stuart this was 'one of those rare moments when you feel in complete control. It doesn't happen very often, but when it does, it just feels good.' Stuart's natural batting style is to attack the bowling: he told me that he 'always had too many shots to be an out-and-out number three,' but *The Times* reported that early on he did not seem at ease when facing Oxford's star bowler, Jamie Dalrymple, though he later batted 'in uninhibited fashion'.

By the end of the first day, Stuart had made 96* off 102 balls in 131 minutes, entering the nineties with one of his three sixes; he had also hit 12 fours. His first partnership in first-class cricket, with Adrian Shankar (143)[104] and which came to an end just before the close, had been worth 159.

---

103 Now Anglia Ruskin University.

104 Shankar later became briefly notorious when, in 2011, his contract with Worcestershire was abruptly terminated after it was alleged that he had made inaccurate claims about his age and playing pedigree.

Ninety-six not out overnight on your first-class debut. 'Did you sleep well?' 'Absolutely' says Stuart. 'If you had said to me at the start of day one that I would be on 96 not out overnight, I think I'd have bitten your arm off. I at no point felt under any pressure – it was just a fantastic day.'

And it carried on in the same vein on day two. He reached his century with an on-drive to the boundary off the very first ball of the day, bowled by Dalrymple, and by lunch had reached 169 off 192 balls, with 17 fours and five straight sixes.

But now, unexpectedly, there was pressure. During the lunch interval, Stuart was told that he was approaching the highest debut-score ever in England.[105] 'All of a sudden, it's a bit like a round of golf when you think you are in danger of scoring a good card, and you start thinking about it' – and first ball after lunch he was, on his own admission, plumb lbw to Australian medium-pacer Ben Vonwiller. His 169 had come out of 317 in 264 minutes.[106]

Cambridge were finally bowled out for 604, at the time a record for this fixture, with Dalrymple taking four for 152 in 52.4 overs. They then bowled well to dismiss Oxford for 224, who were 388 for five (Dalrymple 137) in the follow-on when the game ended as a draw. Stuart did not get his name on the scorecard in any other capacity. He took no catches, and although his medium-pacers had taken a few wickets in his age-group days, a back injury early in his rugby career had already pretty much called time on that aspect of his game.[107]

It was a nine-minute wonder at the time that Stuart had made 169 in what, because he was at the end of his university career and was about to join the pro rugby ranks, was likely to be his only first-class innings. *The Times* even suggested that this was why he was able to bat as he did: Ivo Tennant happily described him as 'batting with all the freedom of one who is no longer tied to his inkwell or batting practice.' Stuart would not disagree.

So it was back to rugby, and for the next six years Stuart made this his career, with cricket getting only a very occasional look-in. Two games for Grange C.C. in the Scottish National Cricket League (SNCL) in 2003, and a duck in his only innings, were his only top-level appearances until 2009. Meanwhile his rugby career had its highs: he won three caps in November 2002, scoring a try on his debut against Romania at Murrayfield, and playing his part in Scotland's famous 21-6 victory over South Africa a week later; and an unexpected recall for a fourth game against Australia in November 2004. But there were lows too – an acrimonious departure from Glasgow at the end of the 2003/04 season, a brief unhappy spell with Castres in 2006/07, and a loss of form after his first three internationals

---

105 At the time, there had been only six higher scores on debut in England than Moffat's 169, the highest of all being Tom Marsden's 227 in 1826, or in more recent times Hubert Doggart's 215* in 1948.

106 This remains the only Varsity Match century for Cambridge by a Scot. The only other century in the fixture by a Scottish-born cricketer was by Lord George Scott for Oxford in 1887. Paul Gibb, of Scottish extraction but born in Yorkshire, made a century for Cambridge in 1938.

107 Stuart returned to bowling in a couple of matches for Grange C.C. in 2011, taking five wickets in the process.

The Cambridge University side of 2002.
Standing (l to r): D.R.Heath, A.Shankar, S.J.Marshall, J.S.D.Moffat,
A.D.Simcox, D.E.T.McGrath, D.J.Noble, J.A.Heath.
Seated: J.R.Moyes (wk), J.W.R.Parker (capt), T.R.Hughes, M.S.Chapman-Smith.
This was the team which played a limited-overs match at Lord's on 25 June, with
Moffat as twelfth man. The first-class fixture, in the Parks, started on 26 June.

which meant he was never in contention for a place in the national side for a Six Nations game, or for a regular international place thereafter.

In the face of such setbacks, gradually Stuart's enjoyment of professional rugby palled. After six seasons at the top level of the game, he retired. Later, he commented: 'When I was an amateur, I just loved playing the game. It was great fun, something that you did before going for a few beers. I don't regret anything I've done or any of the decisions I've made, but professional rugby was grinding me down ... [by the end] my heart just wasn't in it. I was sick of rugby.'[108]

Sick of rugby, at the pro level at least, but not of cricket. For as he told me more than once, 'cricket was always my first love': a remarkable statement from one who had done so well in another sport. In 2009 he returned to the Grange side in the Scottish National Cricket League, scoring 283 runs in his first year back, and improving to 379 in 2010, with a top score of 96; he is still without another top-level century, despite his 100 per cent record in first-class cricket. Not that he has been completely centuryless since 2002: in July 2005 he made 128* out of an innings total of 210 in a festival match to commemorate 150 years of cricket at Raeburn Place. But that 169 remains, so far, the best score of his cricketing life.

Stuart now says: 'Looking back, I would love to have done more in cricket.

---

108   From an article in *The Herald,* 27 September 2009.

I enjoyed rugby but there was always a nagging feeling that if I had committed to cricket it might have been more fitting personality-wise. Rugby was great, but I think professional rugby is something that over the years didn't really stack up to all it might have been. It was good money but my international career never quite got going. I never quite reproduced my club form on the international scene.'

Now that he is back playing cricket, Stuart is happier with his sporting life than for many years: 'I managed half a dozen games [of cricket] throughout my rugby career, and that's why I am enjoying it so much being back involved now. At the weekend we were playing at Grange, it was a beautiful day and the ground couldn't have looked better. It's a pleasure to be there really, which is a feeling I never quite achieved from rugby.'

Sport and the real world
What do they know of life, who only cricket know? Some professional sportsmen and women can be so caught up in the playing careers that occupy the first part of their allotted spans that, when the time comes for them to withdraw from the front line, they have nowhere to go.

Not so Stuart Moffat, who has always been aware of the need to contemplate life without professional sport. Hence his concern to secure academic qualifications and hence, too, the fact that he somewhat fell into professional sport rather than planning in advance to make it a career. As he says, 'When you're a student and somebody offers you a bit of money to play rugby, it's not a hard decision really.' Previously he had been looking for a career that he might be able to combine with rugby: on the eve of his first Varsity match, he had said, 'I want to take things one step at a time. At the moment I hope to get fixed up with a job in Japan next autumn and play a bit of rugby out there. If that leads to something bigger, it will be a bonus.'[109]

Several times during his career, the idea occurred of leaving rugby behind when faced with adversity, and this was not something that fazed him. He told me that after his career-threatening injury in 1999, 'I had pretty much given up rugby, *and was happy to let it go*' [my emphasis]; he was only persuaded back when a phone call from the Cambridge University coach lured him to a place where not only could he resume playing rugby, but he could also acquire further academic qualifications for his life ahead. When his contract with Glasgow Rugby was unexpectedly not renewed in 2004, he was 'contemplating the labour market and seeing how high a standard of amateur rugby he could sustain'. Another source says that at this time he was 'disillusioned by the game in Scotland and seeking a more permanent move down-under.'[110] And when Border Reivers were disbanded on cost grounds in 2007 he says that he 'would have stepped off the professional treadmill,' but an offer from Viadana took him to Italy for one season. For all that he enjoyed his time there, he turned down an offer that would have extended his contract for another year.

---

109   *Daily Record*, 12 December 2000
110   *The Times*, 5 November 2004; *The Scotsman*, 5 November 2004

Stuart Moffat played rugby in Italy for the Lombardy side Viadana in 2007/08.

Asked in mid-2009 how he would react if a call came to rejoin a professional side, his answer was unequivocally in the negative.[111] And when, a year later, I asked him if in ten years' time his rugby days will be behind him, he was equally unequivocal: 'Absolutely.' He has no wish to stay in the game as a manager or coach: 'It's just not me'. But cricket, in ten years' time? 'Still heavily involved. I'd like to be still playing.'

When his pro rugby career finally ended, Stuart had other skills that were – ought to have been – marketable for a career outside sport. A BSc in economics from Loughborough and an MA degree in economics and management from Cambridge ought to have opened doors in his preferred area of banking, finance or investment. 'Unfortunately I finished my rugby career in the middle of a worldwide recession, so looking for a job in investment wasn't ideal timing.' After a period on the jobs market, he found employment for a while in Edinburgh with a head-hunting firm for financial services, but found life at a desk unsatisfying after so long playing rugby. So, as at mid-2011, he was doing some cricket coaching, and looking to invest in a suitable business venture: something that he believes would be more in keeping with his lifestyle.

Stuart's attitude to professional sport – to sport in general – and to its place in a balanced life is one of the reasons why a word sometimes used to describe him is 'Corinthian'. With its associations of amateurism, sport-for-fun, perhaps some suggestion of sport as a diversion for wealthy gentlemen, and some suggestion too of sporting versatility, it suits him well. On the versatility front, as well as cricket and rugby he was a successful squash player in younger days, has aspirations of getting his golf handicap down to scratch, and hopes too to bag a few more Munros as opportunity arises. As for wealthy – well, it's not for me to know or say, but I don't get the impression that the breadline beckons.

But most of all, there's the amateur issue, and the matter of sport for fun. The word 'fun' recurred both in my meetings with Stuart, and in many of the other pieces I've read about him. Rugby – at Cambridge, even at Glasgow – was fun when it was going well; but when things turned trickier, and the grind began, then the fun was lost and it was no longer any pleasure. He says now that, for all that the money in rugby was good, 'it was never about the money – it was always about just playing rugby. I really do think I would have enjoyed it all more if I had been an amateur player.'

While the pressures of professional rugby brought about that loss of fun, this has never been the case with cricket. In the Scottish set-up, there was never any realistic prospect of a career as a professional cricketer, and the

111   The source for this and the quotation at the end of the previous paragraph is an article in *The Herald*, 27 September 2009.

Playing for fun. Stuart Moffat batting for Grange v Uddingston in a Scottish National Cricket League match at Raeburn Place, Edinburgh, in June 2010. (Courtesy of David Potter.)

fact that Stuart was offered good money to become a rugby professional while still at university meant that the idea of a cricket career south of the border never arose. Cricket, therefore, was always 'for fun' – serious fun for sure, but without any of the pressure that arises when your wage-packet depends upon the quality of your performance. It is no coincidence that his 169 for Cambridge University was scored when the pressure was off: his exams were behind him and his immediate future was secured elsewhere.

Now back at Grange, 'it's a pleasure to be there'. Serious club cricket suits him well. Although successful for his club, he has no aspirations to go on to higher things with his cricket, even though time has not yet run out. He told me that he didn't think it was on the cards that he would play again for the national side, although it later emerged that his name has apparently been mentioned as a potential candidate as Cricket Scotland look for a broader player-base for the national Twenty20 side.[112]

And so to the \$169,000 question. If you did get the call to play for Scotland in a first-class match, would the fact that you have an average of 169 to protect play any part in your decision whether to play? Unhesitatingly came the reply, 'No, no, not at all.' Stuart Moffat is well aware of his unusual place in cricket annals, but it is not the statistics that make his one-and-only first-class innings his proudest sporting memory. It was the innings itself – the coming together of circumstances that produced, and enabled him to enjoy, his greatest day.

For all that the University cricket match is now only a shadow of what it once was, and for all that Stuart has four international caps at rugby, one of them won in a historic victory against South Africa, the fact that, for this 'pleasant victim of circumstance' (as he referred to himself), a cricket match in The Parks in June 2002 is his proudest sporting memory tells you – as if you didn't already know it – where his heart really lies.

---

112   *The Herald*, 8 December 2010.

Chapter Five
In the Wickets

An Irish Airman

Robert Gregory is one of only half a dozen bowlers to take eight wickets in an innings in his one and only first-class match. But it is not this that makes him almost certainly the most widely-known of the cricketers covered in this volume; we'll come to that in a while. Brief biographies of him appear in numerous sources, including the *Dictionary of Irish Biography (DIB)*, to which I would refer the reader who is looking for a short but still comprehensive life-history of the man.[113] Here I must concentrate only on the principal features of his life, and – if it is not already regarded as one of those features – on his cricket.

With that in mind, from some of the many sources dealing with Gregory[114] it appears that the main features of his eventful life were these:

- he was born on 20 May 1881 at the family home at Coole Park, near Gort in County Galway
- he was a fine all-round sportsman, whose record includes winning a Blue for boxing and winning the French amateur boxing championship
- he was a leg-spinner who played one first-class match, for Ireland against Scotland in 1912, in which he took eight wickets in Scotland's first innings
- he played non-first-class cricket with W.G.Grace
- he was an outstanding artist and stage-designer, with strong links to the Abbey Theatre in Dublin
- he married a fellow artist in 1906, and they had three children
- in the First World War he became a pilot with the Royal Flying Corps, recording 19 'kills' including shooting down the 'Red Baron'
- he was shot down and killed in action over Italy on 23 January 1918
- he was the subject of, or inspiration for, four post-war poems by W.B.Yeats.

Each of these statements is well-sourced, usually in more than one source. Which makes it all the more remarkable to discover that almost every one of them is to one degree or another wrong, or at best unverifiable.

Let's try and build up an accurate picture of Gregory by examining them one by one.

---

113 *Dictionary of Irish Biography*, ed. James McGuire and James Quinn (Royal Irish Academy/ Cambridge University Press, 2009)

114 Gregory's name is cited in numerous books and articles. Those that have been of most help in preparing this chapter are identified in footnotes or listed in the Bibliography.

Birth

William Robert Gregory was the only child of Sir William Gregory KCMG, sometime MP, member of the Privy Council of Ireland, and Governor of Ceylon, and Lady Augusta Gregory, a major figure in the Irish Literary Revival of the late nineteenth and early twentieth centuries. By birth Lady Gregory was a member of the cricket-loving Persse family,[115] and it is reported that she first met her husband at a cricket match. When they married in 1880, Sir William was 62 and Augusta 27; the *DIB* dismisses rumours that Robert was the outcome of a liaison between Lady Gregory and the local blacksmith.

The family home was certainly at Coole Park, in the western Irish countryside. But though several sources say Robert was born there, they are wrong. The *DIB* gives his place of birth as London, as do Oxford University records, and his birth certificate shows this to be correct: his actual birthplace was the family's central London residence at 3 St George's Place. The property no longer exists, but was located on the south side of Knightsbridge, very close to Hyde Park Corner, approximately where 5 Knightsbridge now stands.

But the birth certificate contains another surprise. Every single source that I have investigated gives Robert Gregory's date of birth as 20 May 1881, and this was the date that he himself gave when entering Oxford University in 1899. But the birth certificate clearly and unequivocally gives his date of birth as 21 May 1881. The informant was Sir William, who ought to have known; though maybe he simply gave the wrong date to the registrar after over-celebrating the birth of his son and heir. But if birth certificates are regarded as the conclusive source on such matters, we must reassign Gregory to a new birthdate of 21 May, as well as to a new place of birth.

Gregory's birth certificate shows he was born in Central London on 21 May rather than in County Galway on 20 May.

This sporting life

Gregory went up to Harrow School at Easter 1895, accompanied by a new cricket bat that his mother had bought for him. It seems he was not an overly industrious student; at Harrow and later at Oxford, the *DIB* describes him as 'talented but lazy; his principal interests were in sport'. He was, it seems, a highly talented allround sportsman, who numbered boxing, riding, hunting and shooting among his interests as well as cricket; and he was successful at all of them. But it seems to have been cricket that predominated. The *DIB* tells that he once claimed that in a dream he

---

115   CricketArchive includes seven cricketers called 'Persse' in its database, including two who played for Irish sides in the 1860s and 1870s.

had been offered the chance to see visions, but turned it down in case it disrupted his cricket playing.

But the tales of his boxing successes are, it seems, frequently exaggerated. Certainly he was a good lightweight boxer, good enough, according to the *DIB*, to have represented New College when he was at Oxford. But I can find no corroboration for the oft-repeated claims that he won a boxing Blue: based on the detailed reports in contemporary issues of *The Times*, he certainly did not fight in any of the Oxford v Cambridge matches in the years that he was at Oxford, or the years immediately following his securing of a third-class degree in 1903.[116] Neither can I find any corroboration that he won the French amateur title. Several sources state that he fought in the French amateur championships, which is plausible – he lived for some years in Paris. Some go as far as saying that he fought for the French lightweight title, which could mean exactly the same thing, or could mean that he reached the final of the event at that weight. Only one source claims that he actually won this title, and on the balance of evidence I would suggest that this is simply wrong; surely if he had done, the other sources would have picked up on the fact?

Leg-spinner for Ireland

CricketEurope states that Gregory narrowly missed selection for the Harrow School cricket eleven but took many wickets for the second team. This may well be true, but I have been unable to corroborate it; surviving records of the period at Harrow are at best patchy. His first definite appearance in an organised match that I have traced is when he appeared for New College Nomads in a match at Headington in May 1901. He was wicketless in this first appearance, but a month later he took six wickets for the Nomads against Blenheim Park at Blenheim. Scores of 16* and 12* in these two games show that he could bat a bit too, even if bowling was his main strength.

The following year, Gregory played twice for the Oxford University Authentics without performing anything special,[117] but he did enough to be selected for a University trial match held in The Parks from 2 to 4 June. Playing for R.S.Darling's XI against W.S.Medlicott's XI, he only took one wicket in the match and scored 9*, but the report in *The Sportsman* after the first day was complimentary: 'Two new men, Bernard and Gregory, were given a trial, and so far the last-named has justified his selection, as although not taking many wickets, he gave distinct promise, getting a good break from leg, with plenty of variety in pitch and pace'.

Nevertheless, he was not called upon again in 1902, and, based on reports in the contemporary sporting press, he played no cricket in his final year at Oxford in 1903; perhaps the prospect of examinations was at last focusing his mind on academic matters. And so passed perhaps his best chance of playing first-class cricket in England.

---

116   Gregory never formally 'took' the BA degree to which he was entitled, and so could not, and did not, style himself 'W.R.Gregory, BA'.

117   In the following winter (1902/03) the Authentics toured India, playing a number of matches that are now regarded as first-class. But the side in India was very different from the sides in which Gregory played in 1902, and it seems unlikely that he was a serious candidate for selection for the tour.

Gregory at a County Galway match in 1909.

From 1904 to 1912, Gregory's name appears spasmodically in reports of cricket matches in Ireland, either for the leading Dublin club, Phoenix, between 1904 and 1912,[118] or for his 'home' club, County Galway, from 1909 to 1912. (Although the name of this latter team looks like that of a county side, Co Galway was in fact no more than a club side, though a good one.) He took 15 wickets in a match, eight for 103 and seven for 94, for Phoenix against Dublin University in July 1908, and ten in a match for Phoenix against Dublin University Long Vacation CC in September 1906. He had his successes with the bat too, scoring 47 and 31 for Phoenix against Leinster in July 1905, and making 60* and 63 in his last two reported innings of 1911, for Co Galway v Grammar School CC, and for Phoenix against Leinster, respectively. In 1909 he played for Co Galway in a famous match against Woodbrook Club and Ground at Bray, south of Dublin, in which one bowler from each side – William 'Budge' Meldon for Co Galway and Ernest Vogler for Woodbrook – took all ten wicket in an innings. In all Vogler took 16 wickets in this match, and scored exactly 100 in his only innings. Gregory's contribution was more modest: scores of 24 and four, and none for 37 while Meldon was running through their opponents' first innings.

In that same year an annual match was instituted between Ireland and Scotland, and following an MCC ruling in 1912 these games are regarded as first-class. The 1912 game was due to begin on 29 August at Leinster's home ground at Rathmines, in Dublin. Three days before that, two of the players selected for the Irish eleven, John Crawfurd and William Pollock, withdrew. In their places, the selectors picked Bill Harrington of Leinster, and Robert Gregory of Co Galway; two surprising replacements, since both were primarily spinners, whereas Crawfurd and Pollock were both primarily batsmen.

Gregory was a reasonable 'form' selection. He had an established track record over the years for Phoenix and Co Galway with both ball and bat; and in his only other reported matches in 1912 he had scored 59 and taken nine wickets in the match for Phoenix against Dublin University at the end of June, and taken three wickets for Co Galway against Na Shuler late in July.

The first day at Rathmines was rained off, which means that Gregory's first-class career began on 30 August rather than 29 August, as is sometimes stated. On 30th, Scotland won the toss and batted, the wicket being described in the *Irish Independent* as 'soft [but] fairly easy till the afternoon was pretty well advanced, when the sun rendered it difficult.' By the end of the first day of play, both sides had completed an innings; Scotland 147 and Ireland, who 'had the worst of the wicket', 98. Gregory

---

118   Cricket Europe is wrong in implying that he first joined Phoenix in 1912 and was promptly catapulted into the Irish team.

scored nought at No.8 but he had entered the record-books by producing a return of 23-2-80-8 in Scotland's innings after opening the bowling. More remarkable still, of his eight wickets three were bowled, two were caught, and one each was lbw, stumped, and hit-wicket, and so in this one innings he had recorded all five of the types of dismissal available to a bowler – a unique feat for anyone playing in his only first-class match.[119]

Unfortunately, newspaper reports in Ireland, Scotland and England tell us almost nothing about the circumstances of any of Gregory's wickets. As was the way in those days, the principal match reports concentrate on the performances of the batsmen, and say little of the bowlers, beyond the *Irish Independent*'s unhelpful 'Gregory carried off the bowling honours, getting eight wickets for 80 runs.'

The third and final day of the game was seriously exciting. Batting a second time, Scotland were bowled out for 83. Harrington took five for 15, another late selection justifying his place, and Gregory 4-1-12-1, coming on surprisingly late as second change, which left Ireland needing 133 to win. From a healthy 93 for four they collapsed to 93 for seven, 99 for eight and 110 for nine. The last pair took them to within four runs of victory before No.11 Paddy Murphy [sic] was bowled, to leave Scotland the winners by three runs. Amidst the mayhem in the 90s Gregory, again at No.8, had been bowled trying a pull shot, to complete a pair, to complete his first-class career, and, so far as I have been able to trace, to complete his competitive cricket career altogether.

So far, then, the facts in the third bullet-point are correct; which leaves only the question of his bowling style. The principal cricket sources agree that he was a leg-spinner; this is supported by the report, quoted above, of his trial match at Oxford. CricketArchive and ESPNcricinfo also credit him with a googly. Other sources refer to him as 'a slow-break bowler' or a bowler of 'medium-paced leg-breaks and cutters'. So far, so reasonably consistent.

But just to confuse things, *The Scotsman*'s report of one of his wickets at Rathmines refers to him bowling one of the Scottish batsmen by 'breaking from the off'; though this could have been a googly, or perhaps the batsman was left-handed.[120] Much greater confusion comes when the usually-reliable *DIB* goes out on its own by describing him as 'an accomplished fast bowler'. So perhaps it's not quite so straightforward after all.

Again, we can only go on the balance of the evidence. I am satisfied that this supports the idea that Gregory was a leg-spinner, very likely with a googly; and probably not the slowest leg-spinner the cricket world has ever seen, either. But as the above evidence has suggested, this is a conclusion than needs to be taken with some caution.

---

119   W.Brown (Tasmania 1857/58) and J.L.Bevan (South Australia 1877/78) each recorded all five forms of dismissal in their only first-class match, but neither did so in the course of a single innings.

120   The principal reference sources do not identify which way round the batsman in question, W.H.Thorburn, batted.

W.G.Grace

Both of the non-cricket brief biographies of Gregory include references to W.G. That compiled by Colin Smythe, see footnote 129, expressly states that Gregory 'played with the legendary W.G.Grace'; this reference is repeated in a letter in Autumn 1989 from Mike Spurrier in *The Cricket Statistician*. The monograph by Roy Clements is however a little more cautious.[121] It includes a photograph which is claimed to show 'the teams of a cricket match at Coole', with both Gregory and W.G. included. But there are more than 22 people in the photograph, and there is no specific statement that W.G. played in the match concerned; indeed, Roy Clements specifically tells us that 'it is said that [W.G.] came [to Coole] more for the out-of season shooting than for the cricket'.

The definitive source on W.G.'s cricket career, J.R.Webber's *The Chronicle of WG*,[122] makes no reference to the great man playing any matches at Coole Park, while Gregory did not play in any of the dozen or so matches elsewhere in Ireland in which W.G. definitely *did* appear. (The relevant scorecards are all in CricketArchive.) So unless Webber has missed any of W.G.'s matches in Ireland, Grace and Gregory never played together in that country. The only other possibility of them playing together would have been for London County, during that side's brief burst of life in the early 1900s. Not in a first-class match, of course: although London County played 64 such matches between 1900 and 1904, W.R.Gregory was never in one of their sides in these games. But the club also played a full programme of minor matches, mostly against South London club sides, in several of which W.G. played. So, can we establish if Gregory ever played in any of these matches with W.G.?

Yes we can, and he didn't. *The Chronicle of WG* doesn't give full scorecards of WG's minor matches, so these have to be tracked down in other sources.[123] Having done so, I can say with certainty that he and Gregory never played in the same London County side. Gregory played only twice in minor matches for London County, both in 1904; these were on 8 June away against Bromley, scoring 2 and taking two for 64, and on 18 June in a home match at Crystal Palace against Guy's Hospital, scoring 40 at No.10 adding 69 for the ninth wicket in less than half an hour with W.M.Banbury, and taking four for 42. Both were, in effect, second eleven matches for the club, and W.G. played in neither of them. At the time of the first match, the 'first eleven' was playing a first-class match against Leicestershire and at the time of the second, they were playing a fixture against Spencer; W.G. played in both these matches. The biggest name that Gregory played alongside in either game was Billy Murdoch, who captained the side against Guy's Hospital. Otherwise he had just two team-mates in each match who were first-class cricketers; the four players concerned accumulated only 21 first-class appearances between them.

---

121   Roy Clements: *Batsman pass by*, Dari Press, 1995
122   J.R.Webber, *The Chronicle of W.G.*, ACS, 1998
123   I am grateful to Joe Webber for pointing me at the best sources for the period in which I am interested.

Artist and stage designer

Alongside his sporting talents, Gregory showed his artistic inclinations early. Soon after leaving Oxford, he greatly pleased his mother (who, it seems, was beginning to despair of him finding a suitable 'career') by announcing his intention of becoming an artist.[124] From 1903 to 1905 he studied at the Slade School of Art in London under Henry Tonks – a widely respected teacher, if something of a tartar in that role. Later he moved to Paris to study under the Anglophile portraitist Jacques-Emile Blanche.

As an artist, Gregory's range was wide. Between 1905 and 1911 he designed sets, costumes and lighting for the Abbey Theatre,[125] painting the sets himself; Colin Smythe's book tells us the theatre's success owed much to his designs. Away from the theatre he painted portraits and 'atmospheric landscapes', as well as turning his hand to smaller-scale exercises such as the design of bookplates. He exhibited his paintings and designs twice in London, at the Baillie Gallery in Bruton Street, Mayfair in 1912, and at the Chenil Gallery in Chelsea in 1914.

At the time at least, his art was well regarded. Blanche said that his work 'reached the highest level of artistic and intellectual merit', while *The Times*, commenting on his 1912 exhibition, said that he 'has a real gift both for landscape and for scenic design ... his pictures are full of the rich and dreamy melancholy that is usually called "Celtic". Many of them are painted in a "Celtic twilight" and [are] haunted by some brooding sadness that is not due to the subjects only ... Mr Gregory is clearly sensitive to several modern movements in art [but] he keeps his own poetic temperament unenslaved.' The same reports in *The Times* give particular praise to his stage designs, which showed him to be 'aware of the need for boldness in construction and reticence in detail'.[126]

Posterity has been less kind to his artistic endeavours. A century later, the *DIB* merely stated that Gregory 'showed some talent as a painter', though it acknowledged that his sets for the Abbey Theatre were 'effective'. Perhaps more pertinently, the article in the *Irish Times* in 2000 already referred to was able to give no more praise to his art than that he 'was obviously a methodical and orderly worker, [but] not especially imaginative or adventurous' and, significantly, concluded that 'It is as much for Robert Gregory's family associations as for the works' own merits that [his] pictures are of interest.'

That that interest persisted into the twenty-first century is shown by the fact that collections of his work were realising sums in the thousands of euro when put up for auction in recent years. But not the sums that would mark him out as an 'outstanding' artist. A collection of 24 of his sketches auctioned in 2006 realised €5,200, against an estimate of €1,500-2,000, while another collection of nine of his watercolours and other sketches

---

124   See article 'Paintings by Lady Gregory's boy in house sale' in the *Irish Times*, 27 May 2000

125   Co-founded in 1904 by Lady Gregory, the Abbey Theatre in Dublin was an early focus of the Irish Literary Revival and of the development of twentieth-century Irish drama - Yeats, Synge, O'Casey, Shaw et al.

126   *The Times*, 11 and 13 June 1912.

auctioned in 2009 realised a disappointing €2,400 against an estimate of €3,000-4,000.[127]

However highly regarded Gregory was as an artist in his lifetime, and for whatever reasons he was so regarded, judged over time perhaps the *DIB*'s modest summation of him as 'showing some talent' in this field is the right one.

Family man

While studying at the Slade, Gregory met Lily Margaret Graham Parry (known as Margaret Parry), a Cheltenham-born fellow student.[128] They later married and had three children: Richard Graham Gregory (1909-1981); Augusta Anne Gregory, later de Winton (1911-2008); and Catherine Frances Gregory, later Kennedy (1913-2000). The children were brought up largely at Coole by their grandmother, while Robert and Margaret were spending much of their time in Paris. Although the Coole estate passed out of the Gregory family in the 1920s, and the house itself was demolished in 1941, it remained the spiritual home of the family, and in their later years his surviving daughters attended an annual gathering at Coole each autumn in honour of their famous grandmother.

Robert's children, understandably, had few memories of their father; the oldest was only seven when their father went off to war. However, they combined to write a foreword to a centenary tribute published in 1981,[129] in which they say that the incidents and impressions that they have gathered of him over the years confirm, for them, Yeats' description of him as 'our perfect man'. Who are we to argue?[130]

The only uncertainty in this section relates to the date of Robert and Margaret's wedding. The *DIB* gives it as 26 September 1906; all other sources give it as 1907, or more specifically as 26 September 1907. The latter date is confirmed by the UK register of births, marriages and deaths. The marriage was at Paddington; their best man was the Welsh painter and draughtsman Augustus John.

After Robert's early death, Margaret as his sole heir was left in charge of the Coole estate. Her attitude towards it differed from that of her prestigious mother-in-law, which created tensions between them. In September 1928, a year after the house was sold, Margaret married Captain Guy Gough of Lough Cutra, close to Coole, who died in 1959; Margaret herself lived on until 1979, when she died in Exeter aged 94.

First World War action

Gregory's ultimately tragic war record, and its literary consequences,

---

127 Details from www.whytes.ie. To be fair, in 2001 his painting 'Burren' realised £11,500 at auction, according to an article on Robert Gregory at www.pgil-eirdata.org.
128 Margaret was of American extraction; some sources incorrectly give her place of birth as Cobham, Virginia.
129 *Robert Gregory 1881-1918: A Centenary Tribute* (edited and published by Colin Smythe, 1981)
130 However, an essay by James Pethica, 'Yeats's Perfect Man', published in the Dublin Review No.35 in summer 2009, casts serious doubt on this description of Gregory.

Gregory in flying kit in 1916.

could be the subject of a book on their own; but here I must keep it brief.

He was commissioned into the 4th Battalion of the Connaught Rangers in September 1915, but wanting more action than this reserve battalion could offer, he began training to join the Royal Flying Corps the following January. Although old for a wartime aviator – he was already 34 – his short stature and the facts that he was 'physically slight but by no means delicate'[131] and a quick learner made him well suited to this arduous role. Between August 1916 and July 1917 he spent a continuous 11 months in action as a scout pilot with 40 Squadron, including missions over the Somme and Ypres fronts; his long survival is testament to his flying skills. He escaped uninjured when his FE8 was shot down on 25 September 1916,[132] and in the summer of 1917 he was awarded the Military Cross and the Legion d'Honneur for his achievements; the MC citation noted that he had 'invariably displayed the highest courage and skill'.

In mid-1917 he transferred to 66 Squadron, and he took command of the squadron in mid-October shortly before it moved from France to the Italian front in November 1917. Sadly, his good luck could not last indefinitely, and on 23 January 1918 Major Gregory, as he now was, lost his life when his plane crashed near Padua.

More information on his career as an aviator can be found in many sources. For present purposes, we must just consider in a bit more detail three of the more mysterious aspects of his flying career, as reported in at least some of those sources.

First, as noted earlier, several authorities, including the *DIB*, credit him with 19 'victories' over enemy aircraft during his flying career. If correct, this would make him one of the leading Allied aces of the First World War. Yet his name does not appear in the list of aces – defined as those with five or more 'kills' or 'victories' to their credit – in published records, including the comprehensive and definitive study *Above the Trenches*.[133]

From records in the National Archives I can identify only two probable 'victories' during Gregory's time with 40 Squadron, from five combat reports bearing his name dated between February and May 1917, and none during his time with 66 Squadron.[134] Even if some reports have not survived, it seems that a figure of 'under five' victories is much more likely

---

131   Adrian Smith, *Major Robert Gregory and the Irish Air Aces of 1917-18*, on www.historyireland.com

132   Trevor Henshaw, *The Sky Their Battlefield*, Grub Street, 1995.

133   Christopher Shores, Norman Franks and Russell Guest, *Above the Trenches*, Grub Street, 1990.

134   National Archives refs AIR1/1222/204/5/2634 (40 Squadron Air Combat Reports from September 1916) and AIR1/1575/204/80/76 (66 Squadron record books December 1917 to March 1918).

than the 19 with which he is sometimes credited. But if this is so, how come the citation for his MC states that '*On many occasions* [my emphasis] he has, at various altitudes, attacked and destroyed or driven down hostile machines'?[135] There's a continuing mystery here that needs the research of a more adept military historian than the present writer to resolve.

And what of Gregory *vs* the Red Baron? None of the sources that allude to Gregory shooting down Manfred von Richthofen claims unequivocally that he did so, yet the mere fact that this was a possibility is intriguing.

In fact, von Richthofen was only shot down once, on 6 July 1917; and Gregory most certainly was not involved in that incident. But four months earlier, on 9 March, the Red Baron had been forced to land, under control, after his fuel tanks were holed as a result of fire from an FE8 of 40 Squadron; and more than one reputable source states that Gregory was 'probably' the pilot concerned.[136] The distinction between being 'shot down' and 'forced down under control' may seem a minor one, but a distinction was certainly drawn at the time: by this stage of the war the latter would not have been scored as a 'victory'. As a matter of fact, therefore, it is wrong to say that Gregory either actually or possibly 'shot down' the Red Baron, even though he *may* have caused him to end one of his missions prematurely. And from the fact that we know that von Richthofen was back in the air later on 9 March, albeit in a different aircraft, it is clear that his downing on that day was of no great significance, military or otherwise; whether or not Gregory was directly responsible, which we can never know.[137]

Finally, we come to the circumstances of Gregory's death. There is consensus nowadays that he was shot down in error by an Italian plane during a test flight,[138] in what today would be called a friendly fire incident. So, 'killed in action' perhaps; but not in combat. At the time of his death, his family was told that he passed out at the controls of his Sopwith Camel because of an adverse reaction to a recent immunisation; this was almost certainly a cover-up. The date of 23 January 1918 is confirmed in contemporary sources, but the place of death may not have been the usually-cited location of 'Grossa, near Padua' (which is where 66 Squadron was based): the squadron history states that his plane was found as 'a complete wreck' at Monastiero, which is a hamlet around 15 km north-east of Grossa, and 30 km north of Padua. So it seems that the recorded place of Gregory's death, as well as that of his birth, will need to be changed.

Robert Gregory was, by all accounts, a successful and popular pilot. He was also, despite the risks of his job, a contented one. The *DIB* and his centenary tribute record that it was as an airman that he truly found himself. He is reported as telling George Bernard Shaw that his combat

---

135   *The Times*, 19 July 1917.

136   Peter McManus, *Richthofen Jagdstaffel Ahead,* Grub Street, 2008; and the essay by James Pethica cited earlier.

137   There is no combat report in Gregory's name for 9 March 1917. The suggestion in Gerald Siggins and James Fitzgerald's *Ireland's 100 Cricket Greats* (Nonsuch Publishing, 2006) that Gregory died the day after he was 'believed to have shot down the famous Red Baron' is simply wrong.

138   His death is reported in these terms in the near-contemporary *History of 66 Squadron*, National Archives ref AIR1/694/21/20/66.

experience had been the happiest period of his life, and a friend who met him at that time commented that Gregory evidently meant this: 'To a man with his power of standing up to danger – which must mean enjoying it – war must have intensified his life as nothing else could; he got a grip of it that he could not through art or love.'[139]

Gregory and Yeats

W.B.Yeats was a great friend and close colleague of Lady Gregory, Robert's mother, and was a regular and often long-term house-guest at Coole Park. For Robert, sometimes too long-term; and by the First World War he had had more than enough of Yeats' presence at his home.

Nevertheless, after Robert's death and at Lady Gregory's prompting,[140] Yeats memorialised him in the writing of four poems: 'Shepherd and Goatherd', 'In memory of Major Robert Gregory', 'An Irish airman foresees his death', and 'Reprisals'. The last of these was withheld, at Lady Gregory's request, until after Yeats' death. So at least, this is one of the bullet-points at the start of this chapter that is incontrovertibly accurate.

It is the third of these poems, a single verse of 16 lines, that is best remembered today. It contains no express mention of Robert Gregory, and for that reason it is 'An Irish airman' rather than 'Robert Gregory' who is known through the poem today. Or, in the happy words of his Cricket Europe entry it is through this poem that Gregory 'is known, if not by name, to generations of poetry enthusiasts and school students – not always the same thing.'[141]

All four poems can be readily found in anthologies or on the internet. I have neither the space nor the expertise to discuss them here, nor to assess whether what they imply about Robert Gregory's life and attitudes was accurate, or were just the musings of a poet seeking to present wider truths than merely the attitudes of one man. However, for all that Yeats was well acquainted with Gregory before the War, and for all the intrinsic merits of the poems as poetry, my suspicion is that they should not necessarily be taken at face value as giving us an unqualified insight into the character of Robert Gregory himself.[142]

But has any other first-class cricketer ever inspired such a number of poems from such a distinguished poet?

Summing up

If ever a man's life contained enough material for a full-length biography, it was surely Robert Gregory's. Into a mere 36 years and 8 months he crammed a wide range of highly diverse activities, and moreover achieved a considerable degree of success at pretty much all of them; and his memory is further enshrined through four poems written in his honour

---

139   Henry Lamb RA, quoted in *Robert Gregory 1881-1918: A Centenary Tribute.*

140   There is much more on the background to the writing and reception of these poems in the essay by James Pethica cited earlier.

141   I gather that in practice this poem is not now, and has not been in the past, part of the regular syllabus for all Irish students, but that those who have studied Yeats in any depth will certainly be familiar with it.

142   James Pethica's essay addresses this point further.

by one of his country's leading poets. Yet today he is still better known as his mother's son than in his own right as a sportsman, or an artist, or an aviator; or, indeed, as a remarkable combination of all three.

The *DIB* refers to Yeats' opinion that Gregory, 'though possessing considerable talent, was dilettantish and lacked direction'. But one man's dilettante is another's Renaissance Man, and that is certainly how he is remembered by his admirers today: 'a Renaissance figure whose early death might have been an illustration for the maxim that whom the gods love die young'.[143]

Cricket was clearly only a very minor activity in Gregory's life, although as a young man it was undoubtedly important to him. Had he survived the Great War, he would surely have been too old to have resumed a career at first-class level, even if the spirit had been willing – which, after his intense wartime activities, might have been doubtful. It is no bad thing that cricket-lovers remember him, if only for an unlikely bowling performance in his only first-class game. But let them never forget that that performance was just a passing moment in the life of one who deserves a fuller – and more accurate – recording and assessment of his life-story than he has been accorded in one place to date.

Another Eight-For

Although Robert Gregory is, for obvious reasons, the star of this chapter, we must consider also the only other Briton to take eight wickets in an innings in his only first-class match. First, here is the full list of those achieving this feat:

Eight wickets in an innings in only first-class match

W.Brown	Tasmania v Victoria	Hobart	1857/58	7-42, 8-31
H.W.Hole	Nelson v Wellington	Nelson	1874/75	8-37, 2-24
J.L.Bevan	South Australia v Tasmania	Adelaide	1877/78	6-23, 8-36
W.R.Gregory	Ireland v Scotland	Dublin	1912	8-80, 1-12
H.M.Hinde	Minor Counties v Leveson Gower's XI	Eastbourne	1924	8-77, 1-61
V.Thambuswamy	Madras v Andhra Pradesh	Guntur	1967/68	1-20, 8-37

In parallel with Michael Harbottle in Chapter Four, the only Englishman in this list was a military man whose most senior cricket was played at Minor Counties level, when his other duties permitted. His was, however, a rather more orthodox military life.

Again like Harbottle, **Harold Montague Hinde** came from a military family. Born at Southsea on 24 August 1895, he was the second of four

---

143 From an undated (?1982) review by Janet Madden-Smith in *Books Ireland* (accessible via www.colinsmythe.co.uk) of *Robert Gregory 1881-1918: A Centenary Tribute.*

children of William Hinde (later Lt-Colonel in the Royal Engineers) and his wife Mildred, née Ilott.[144] By 1909 the family was living at Crowthorne, Berkshire, in a house owned by nearby Wellington College, where William had been a pupil in the 1870s, and where Harold began as a day boy in January 1909. After a year at Wellington, Harold's education mysteriously shifted to Blundell's School in Devon. I'd like to think that there is some slightly sinister, or at least slightly mischievous, reason for this move, but I suspect that it was something more prosaic: perhaps his parents just felt he would be better served by boarding at a school well away from home.

Details of Hinde's academic record have not survived, but he was evidently a strong and versatile sportsman, reaching the Blundell's School first teams in rugby, cricket and hockey, and also distinguishing himself in tennis, swimming and diving. His physical strength was shown when he won the 'throwing the cricket ball' event at Blundell's in 1913 with the remarkable distance, for a 17-year-old, of 113 yards 2½ inches.

In the autumn of 1913 he went to the Royal Military College at Sandhurst, back close to the family home, and his military career began in earnest when he was commissioned into the Royal Army Service Corps (or ASC as it then was) a fortnight after the outbreak of the First World War. He served throughout the war in France and Belgium, apart from a brief period in 1915 when he was invalided home, and as well as being once mentioned in dispatches he was, in 1919, awarded the OBE for his war service.

Ready to play.
Hinde in 1913.

He continued his military career at home until 1924, when he was posted to Egypt where he stayed until 1930. After more time on the home front he served in Palestine from 1936 to 1938. He spent the Second World War in senior posts in Supplies and Transport in Norway, France, Belgium, North Africa and Italy, receiving four more mentions in dispatches (two in 1940, two in 1945) and being awarded the CBE in 1943 in recognition of his 'sound planning, execution and organising ability [and] work of a consistently high order'. For his wartime services he also received decorations from the USA (Officer of the Legion of Merit, and Bronze Star), Luxembourg (Commander of the Order of Couronne de Chene) and France (Chevalier of the Legion d'Honneur).

After the war he spent a period as commandant of the RASC School at Aldershot, before spending his last three years in the Army as Director of Supplies and Transport for the Middle East Land Forces. From 1947 he was also an *aide de camp* to the King, not quite as distinguished a post as it sounds, but nevertheless a fine reward for an honourable military career. He retired from the Army in September 1950 just after his 55th birthday. For his long and distinguished services, Brigadier Hinde, as he had become

---

144   I have been unable to establish any link with the family of a more famous cricketing Ilott.

in 1948, was awarded the CB in the Birthday Honours in 1951.

Thereafter he lived in retirement initially in England, and later at the house of his widowed sister Elsie at Santa Margherita Ligure in Italy, on the Riviera di Levante coast just east of Genoa, where he died suddenly on 16 November 1965 at the age of 70.[145]

So cricket and other sports had to fit round a busy military career. Hinde's main winter sport in his younger days was rugby – he was a forward for Richmond and the Army between 1919/20 and 1923/24, and played in three England trials. He certainly had the physique for it: he was over six feet in height and described as 'well built'; but at the same time, he was also said to be 'graceful in movement'.[146]

In the summer, when opportunity permitted, he played cricket. He had emerged as a fast bowler in his last year at Blundell's, taking eight for 19 in 13 overs in one school match in 1913. The report of the school's season described him as 'fast right-hand, with an easy natural action. A hard-working bowler who keeps a dangerous length, and if he is unlucky in not getting wickets, cannot often be scored off easily.' He was less distinguished in other aspects of the game: his batting was never anything to write home about,[147] and the report of the Blundell's 1912 season was unequivocal about his performance in the third key element: 'not a good field, slow in getting down to the ball, and does not cover any ground.'

After the First World War, he played with success in military matches and in 1921, qualifying through his Crowthorne connections, he made the first of his 34 Minor Counties appearances for Berkshire. At the end of that season he took five for 33 in the first innings of the Championship challenge match against Staffordshire, in which Berkshire were almost certainly deprived of the title by rain. He was a regular in their side for the next three years – including in 1924, when the county took the title by winning the challenge match against Northumberland.

But his best season was 1923. In eight matches in the Minor Counties competition he took 56 wickets, including innings returns of eight for 114 against Devon and eight for 78 against Cornwall, and twice taking ten or more wickets in a match. To this day, only four other bowlers have taken more wickets in a season for Berkshire, and only one has done so when playing in fewer matches. His immediate reward was a place in the Minor Counties (South) side against Minor Counties (North) at The Oval at the end of August, in which Buckinghamshire's Frank Edwards took 14 wickets; at the other end, Hinde took four of the other six.

---

145   In another parallel with Michael Harbottle, Hinde's two brothers had both succumbed in the First World War. The younger, Lt Cyril de Villiers Hinde, was killed in action near Ypres in July 1917 at the age of 19; the older, Capt William Henry Rousseau Hinde, died in hospital at Leeds, aged 27, in the influenza epidemic in October 1918. W.H.R.Hinde played five Minor Counties matches for Berkshire in 1913 and 1914, scoring 58 runs at an average of 5.80, highest score 21, and not bowling.

146   From Hinde's obituary in *The Waggoner*, the RASC/RCT in-house journal.

147   A report in the Berkshire Yearbook for 1956, cited in full later, states that his lack of skill as a batsman was 'in consequence of a blinded eye'. I have no reason to doubt that he may have suffered from this disability, but I have seen no reference to it in any other source.

His 1923 performances earned Hinde a place in the Minor Counties side that played H.D.G.Leveson Gower's XI at Eastbourne at the end of June 1924, in what was to be the Counties' first first-class match since the war, and only their second ever.

This was the first senior match of Hinde's season, but he showed no signs of rustiness. After the Minor Counties had been dismissed in around three hours for 143 (Hinde 0*), they reduced Leveson Gower's side to 129 for nine by the close of the first day, with Hinde having taken seven for 61, six of them bowled. He finished off the innings with his eighth wicket, caught, early on the second day. Contemporary newspaper reports concentrate on the speed of his bowling: according to the *Eastbourne Gazette* G.E.V.Crutchley 'had his stumps scattered by a straight fast one from Hinde', W.H.G.Heath was 'obviously puzzled by the fast deliveries of Hinde' before eventually 'falling a victim to a beautiful ball from Hinde which sent the bails spinning', and Ernest Smith 'appeared to be settling down to a good score when one of his stumps was removed by a fast ball from Hinde'.

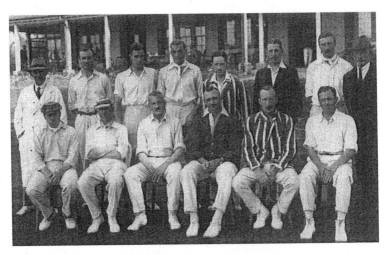

The Aldershot Command side of 1924.
Standing (l to r): W.H.Harborne (umpire), C.C.Haynes, O.C.Adams, H.M.Hinde, T.E.M.Battersby, A.A.Durand, D.W.C.Ray, T.E.Clarkson (scorer).
Seated: P.V.Williams, B.F.Clarke, J.S.Bostock, E.L.W.Henslow, J.W.T.Priestman, F.R.S.Shaw.

Pace and accuracy seem to have been Hinde's watchwords, for a high proportion of 'bowled' dismissals in an innings was nothing new to him. In his Minor Counties career he took almost 42 per cent of his wickets in this way.

After conceding a first-innings lead of four runs, the Minor Counties second time around exactly doubled their first-innings total – Hinde scored a duck – leaving their opponents a target of 283. Hinde took the first wicket of their second innings (bowled), but the batsmen seemed to have more of his measure this time, and it was left to Frank Edwards and A.G.Doggart to bowl the Counties to victory in a thrilling finish by just two runs.

After this, the wet 1924 season was an anti-climax for Hinde. He took only nine wickets in five matches in the Minor Counties competition – the Berkshire club's annual report said that he never had a wicket to suit him – and now military duties took him off to Egypt. He returned to the Berkshire side for two matches in 1926, almost a full season in 1930, and a final hurrah in the Challenge match of 1932, a rain-ruined game that left Bucks as the competition winners. But as much as anything because of his long periods of absence from Britain, he was never again a contender for a place in a first-class side.[148]

He was still playing cricket, though. Army sides in Egypt between the wars played to a good standard, notably against visiting sides such as the Free Foresters and the teams led by H.M.Martineau who toured annually between 1929 and 1939. Hinde played in four matches against the Free Foresters in 1927, taking 18 wickets in the six innings in which he bowled, including 12 in the two matches for 'All-Egypt' against the tourists. In one of these matches he surprised probably even himself by scoring a hard-hit 27*, at his proper place at eleven, the highest of only five double-figure scores in the 58 innings recorded for him in CricketArchive.[149] According to *The Cricketer*, during this tour 'Hinde bowled well and his fielding at mid-off was also excellent', something that no doubt would have surprised his erstwhile coaches at Blundell's. He also played against Martineau's XI in Egypt in 1930 in three matches, taking nine wickets, before returning home for his last nearly-full season for Berkshire. During that 1930 season he also turned out for The Quails, described in *The Cricketer* as 'the I Zingari of Egypt', against the Free Foresters on Martineau's own ground at Holyport near Maidenhead and took six for 39 in the Foresters' first innings.

After his brief return for the big match of the 1932 Minor Counties season, other duties seem to have kept Hinde away from serious cricket. As far as Berkshire were concerned, however, it was a case of 'gone but not forgotten'. In an article entitled *Berkshire Cricket Memories* by Major Guy Bennett in the mid-1950s – and reprinted in the yearbook for 1999 – we read that 'Among other between-war cricketers who played for the county with much success ... was also Captain H.M.Hinde, known as "Satan" ...'.

Quite a nickname for a soldier to bear, for it seems he wasn't just known as Satan in cricketing circles. The name is included in the family notice of his death in *The Times*, alongside an apparent second nickname of Mike,

---

148   A representative Minor Counties XI played seven further first-class matches between 1924 and Hinde's last Berkshire match in 1932; meanwhile the Army were playing between two and four first-class matches each season. But Hinde did not find a place in any of these sides.

149   His batting performances for Berkshire deserve a little elaboration. He made double-figures only three times in 41 innings with scores of 11 and 20 in 1923, and 14 in 1930. He was scoreless in 21 of those innings with ten ducks and 11 scores of 0*. He did not score a run in his seven innings in 1922, and including the last match of 1921 he went eight matches, and eight innings, without a run.

though curiously, neither Mike nor Satan is included in the otherwise similarly-worded notice in the *Daily Telegraph*. He is also referred to as 'Satan' Hinde in his obituary in *The Waggoner*. However this nickname came about, it should not be taken at face value as an indicator of Hinde's character. Forceful and a strict disciplinarian, certainly. But also a man who was loyal to his Corps and his friends, and devoted to his duty; who was 'one of the Corps' more celebrated personalities, [who] always created a team spirit and got the best out of those serving under him through his personality. A leader in the true sense of the word'; and who had 'a sympathetic and kindly nature which made him beloved by all who served under him.'[150]

But not, perhaps, by all those who had to face his fast bowling.

Three in a row

OK, so six bowlers have taken eight in an innings on debut and never played first-class cricket again. But only one can claim to have taken a hat-trick in his only match at this level.

Northamptonshire's fixture against the touring side from Dublin University in July 1925 was seen by the county club as an opportunity to try out a few new players, and to give a rest to some of their Championship regulars. Of the eleven who took the field on the first day of the game, three were making their first-class debuts, two others had three first-class appearances between them, another had seven, and even the captain only had 14. Among the relative newcomers were two bowlers from the Kettering Town club: Edgar Towell, who had played a single first-class match for the county in 1923, and debutant **Dick Wooster**.[151]

Wooster, christened Reginald but always known as Dick, was a Kettering man from first to last. He was born there on 19 January 1903, lived all his life there, and died there on 12 September 1968, aged only 65. For many years between the wars he was a stalwart of the Kettering Town club, principally as a medium-paced bowler, though he made the occasional good score with the bat too. The club history[152] refers to the 1920s as 'flourishing years indeed', and names Wooster as one of the dominant players of the era, along with the many members of the Wright family,[153] Edgar Towell, George Johnson (who played 18 matches for Northamptonshire between 1922 and 1932) and John Lamb (who had 38 county matches in the thirties).

---

150 Quotations taken from *The Waggoner*'s reports of his retirement and, later, his death.

151 Another member of the Northants side was Norman Bowell, who had made his first-class debut for Hampshire the previous season alongside Fred Hyland (qv).

152 Peter Larcombe, *A Century of Cricket at Kettering: 1885-1985*, Kettering Town CC, 1985.

153 Nine different cricketers with the surname Wright made their debuts for Northamptonshire between 1919 and 1923. Seven were made up of two sets of brothers (cousins to each other), all from Kettering. The other two were also brothers, from Northampton, but they were not related to the 'Kettering Seven'.

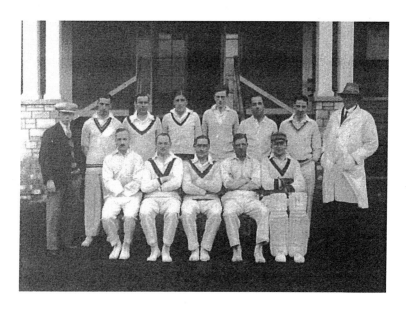

At home. The Kettering CC eleven in 1927 in front of their pavilion then under construction. Standing (l to r): L.Marshall (scorer), C.W.Miller, F.C.Thompson, R.Wooster, T.H.M.Preston, S.Wright, M.A.James, A.H.Lea (umpire). Seated: W.H.Cawton, W.C.Farnsworth, E.F.Towell (capt), H.J.Parker, G.H.Johnson (wk). Wooster and three of his teammates played county cricket.

Wooster wasn't exactly sweeping all before him in club games in 1925: over the season as a whole he took just 31 wickets for the club, at an average of 11.33. But he had nevertheless caught the eye of the county club, and his cause cannot have been harmed when he took six wickets for Kettering against Rothwell at the end of June. So the Dublin University game was an opportunity to have a closer look at him.

This was the last, and only first-class, match of the University's short tour to England; but if they had saved their best till last, then I'm afraid their best was nowhere near good enough, as they were comprehensively beaten by what amounted to an 'A' eleven of one of the weaker first-class counties. The University batted first when the game began on Saturday, 18 July and were dismissed by 3.25 pm for 197, rugby international Mark Sugden top-scoring with 36. Dick Wooster was the fourth bowler used in the innings, and took his only wicket when he bowled No.7, James Wills, in his seventh over, to make the University 169 for eight. Wooster bowled nine overs in the innings, returning 9-1-23-1 in two spells. Unfortunately my attempts to interpret the scorebook[154] have not established beyond doubt whether he bowled to Samuel Beckett, who was one of the University's six first-class debutants, and who scored 18 in as many minutes, with four fours, batting at No.8, but he may very well have done so.

---

154   The scorebook now resides at the Northamptonshire Record Office.

By the end of the first day the county had made 173 for four, and on the Monday they extended this to a final total of 396, with best scores of 83 by P.A. 'Bill' Wright and 71 by opener Wilfrid Timms. Wooster, at No.10, scored six – two twos and two singles – before giving a straightforward caught-and-bowled back to James Wills; in his 15-minute stay he helped to add 41 with Bill Wright.

The University batted again, needing 199 to make the county bat a second time. Their innings began at 3.10 pm, and three minutes later Wooster, asked this time to open the attack, bowled Achey Kelly with his first ball of the innings. Around twenty minutes later he bowled Mark Sugden, and after five overs his figures were 5-0-17-2. And now glory beckoned. The first five balls of his sixth over comprised three dots and two boundaries, but with his sixth he had Joseph Peacocke caught by his captain, John Fitzroy, for 10. Edgar Towell bowled the next over, in which opener George McVeagh and the new batsman Charles McCausland scored three runs, and then it was Wooster's turn again. With the first ball of his seventh over he bowled McVeagh for 17, and next ball he bowled Wills for the second time in the match. The University were now 56 for five, and Wooster's figures had improved to 6.2-0-25-5, including a hat-trick. According to the scorebook, Wooster's glory moment – the third wicket of his hat-trick – had come at 3.51 pm precisely.

X marks the spot. The Northamptonshire scorebook, showing Wooster's hat-trick against Dublin University at Northampton in July 1925. (Courtesy of Northamptonshire Record Office.)

Local newspaper reports do not record what level of celebration, if any, there was of Wooster's feat, but it certainly did not go unnoticed, as it was referred to in all match reports the following day. Whether the excitement of the achievement then got to him, or whether the batsmen just got his measure, we don't know, but he was wicketless for his remaining 6.4 overs, in which he conceded 29 runs, including 14 in his 11th over. James Pigot, whose 49 was to be the University's top score of the match, scored 13 runs off this over, including three fours. Wooster's final analysis was 13-1-54-5; the Northamptonshire scorebook indicates that this was bowled in a single spell, though the *Northampton Daily Chronicle* says that his rough treatment by Pigot came in 'a second spell'. I prefer to believe the scorebook.

The bowling of Bill Wright and Graham Norris, another debutant, took care of the remaining University batsmen. The side was dismissed for 143 at about 5.30 pm, leaving the county winners by an innings and 56 runs; at which point Dick Wooster walked off the first-class field for ever, no doubt to a further round of back-slapping from his team-mates, and a further smattering of applause from the assembled multitude. (Or however many people there were at Wantage Road at 5.30 pm on the second scheduled day of a non-Championship match.)

Two days later Northants were back to the merry-go-round of the Championship, with a match against Yorkshire at – as it happened – the Town Ground at Kettering. Only the six most experienced members of the side that had beaten Dublin University were in the county side for this game; in fact, none of the three who had made their debuts against the University, and neither of the two players who had only played one or two first-class matches before that game, played again for Northamptonshire in 1925. But apart from Wooster and, as noted earlier, Norman Bowell, all had another chance for the county later. Indeed, opener W.C.Brown, who had made his first-class debut in the match against Dublin University, went on to play a further 126 first-class matches; and Edgar Towell, who had one match before the University game, played a further 68 matches. Both became regulars for the county from 1928.

But not Wooster. His daughter, Anne Parkinson, has told me that her father was subsequently invited to play more regularly for the county but, probably under some parental pressure, decided that he could not afford to give up his position in the drawing office of a building firm in Kettering. So the Dublin University game remained his only first-class match; and the decision not to play again for the county has led to his unique position in the record-books today. It is good to be able to report that his feat did not go unremarked by the county club, who subsequently presented him with the hat-trick ball, suitably mounted and inscribed; it remains today a proud possession in the Parkinson household.

Dick Wooster shared memorable moments off the cricket field as well as on it. Notably, he was in Normandy on the second day of the D-Day landings. He married Kate Anne (Kath) O'Rourke in Kettering in 1934, and they had a son, another Dick, as well as daughter Anne. His love of cricket remained throughout his life, and has been passed on to his son, grandsons, and a great-grandson. Perhaps one day another Wooster, or a Parkinson, will emerge on the first-class scene to take on the mantle of their distinguished forebear.

Two points remain. First the status of 'Wooster's Match': was it really a first-class fixture, given the relative weakness of both sides? The answer is, unequivocally, yes. Its recognition as a first-class match derives largely, it would seem, from the fact that *Wisden* treated it as such in 1926, as it did a handful of other matches between Dublin University and English counties in the 1920s. Mind you, that status wasn't obvious from the outset: in *The Cricketer* the match score was given, without any report or bowling figures, not on the pages devoted to first-class inter-county matches, but in the section headed 'Club Matches', where it appears between the scorecards of Mitcham v Honor Oak, and Chiswick Park v Ealing.[155]

---

155   *The Cricketer*, 8 August 1925, p 443.

Even today, and despite the ACS's inclusion of it in its first-class match-list, there are some who are less sure about the game's status. I have correspondence dated October 2010 from the Northamptonshire CCC archivist in which he writes that Wooster's match 'was not deemed as [a] first-class game ... [Wooster] did take a hat-trick, but of course this was not recognised.' Well, as we have seen, it was recognised by the county club at the time, and the game has been fully accepted as a first-class match for many years. But it is true that his hat-trick took some time to find its way into the record books: it is not included in the list of hat-tricks in the first edition of Roy Webber's *Playfair Book of Cricket Records* in 1951, though it made it into the next edition of that book, in 1961, with the bowler unfortunately mis-identified as G.Wooster, but we'll let that pass.[156]

And finally, Wodehousians will spot the resonance of Dick Wooster's name, and may wonder. It is well known that Bertie Wooster's gentleman's gentleman Jeeves was named after the pre-First World War Warwickshire cricketer Percy Jeeves. In 1971, late in his writing career, cricket-lover P.G.Wodehouse revealed that 'his' Jeeves's first name was Reginald: the same as the given name of our Dick Wooster. Could it be that he chose this Christian name as an allusion to the Northamptonshire cricketer, whose name somehow stuck with Wodehouse for over 45 years after the day that secured his fame?

It would be lovely to think so, but I fear the answer is no. Wodehouse's first writings about a Bertie Wooster-like character appeared in some short stories written before the First World War; the character concerned was named Reginald Pepper. If Wodehouse's decision to christen 'his' Jeeves as Reginald was made with any backward glance - and there is no reason to assume that it was - then Reggie Pepper is surely more likely to have been the inspiration, rather than our Reginald Wooster. But you never know ...

---

156   His name was not finally corrected in the major record books until the second edition of the *Wisden Book of Cricket Records* in 1986.

Chapter Six

First Ballers, and a Mystery

Not every bowler begins with a wide to second slip.

It must be every debutant bowler's dream to settle their nerves by taking a wicket with the very first ball they bowl. In first-class cricket, over 100 cricketers have done so, including such later-famous names as Colin Blythe, Bill Alley and Paul Collingwood. They have had some famous victims too – indeed, Geoffrey Boycott and Mark Taylor were both out twice to an opponent's first-ever first-class delivery.[157] Some of the bowlers may have been a little fortunate in the way their secured their first-ball wickets: for example, both D.H.Mitchell (Transvaal, 1954/55) and S.Srivastava (Delhi, 1984/85) did so by means of a 'hit-wicket' dismissal. But all must have hoped that, after such a good start, they had earned a run in the side, to have the chance to show whether their early success was just a flash in the pan, or something rather more.

So it comes as a surprise to find that at least eight of those achieving this feat never played another first-class match.

Wicket with first ball in only first-class match

F.W.Wingrove	Victoria v Australian XI	Melbourne	1885/86	2-58, dnb
J.Johns	Glamorgan v Somerset	Cardiff	1922	2-29, 0-33
F.Buttner	OFS v Western Province	Cape Town	1923/24	4-56, 1-56
J.Lee	Leicestershire v Glamorgan	Cardiff	1947	1-13, dnb
K.R.Flint	Tasmania v MCC	Launceston	1965/66	3-133, 3-93
R.L.Biffin	Tasmania v Indians	Hobart	1967/68	2-5, 0-16
Fawad Usman	Pakistan Universities v United Bank	Peshawar	1978/79	1-11, 0-24
H.Harry	Punjab v Baroda	Vadodara	1998/99	1-8

I say 'at least eight', because there is another name absent from that list, which perhaps should – and perhaps shouldn't – be added to it. This chapter is, mostly, his story. It is, as we will see, a story involving a deal of uncertainty.

---

157   Boycott to A.R.Frost (South Australia, 1965/66) and C.Lethbridge (Warwickshire, 1981), and Taylor to A.L.Penberthy (Northamptonshire, 1989) and P.T.McPhee (Tasmania, 1989/90). Boycott was one of three members of the MCC team in Australia in 1965/66 to fall victim to an opponent's first first-class delivery.

Ely's Mr Chips

Francis William Wilkinson, 'F.W.' or, to generations of schoolboys, 'Wilkie', was a north-easterner, born on 4 October 1895 at Norton-on-Tees in County Durham, near Middlesbrough. His family background seems to have been relatively humble: his father was a joiner in the building trade. Nevertheless, Francis was educated at Middlesbrough High School before, late in 1915, he joined the Machine Gun Corps. He served at home and in France until his demob in January 1919, winning the Military Medal in 1918 for bravery under fire, 'showing extreme indifference to personal danger'.

Later in 1919 he secured entry to Clare College, Cambridge, where he took his BA degree in 1922. At Cambridge, sport seems to have been at least as important to him as his studies, for he received no more than an 'ordinary' classics degree, but won three Blues at two different sports; neither of which was cricket.

He played no first-class cricket at Cambridge, and neither did he appear in any of the main trial matches, though he became a member of the Crusaders club. A possibly mis-spent youth was in evidence when he won a Blue for billiards in March 1921, captaining his side to an easy win over Oxford. But his principal sport at the University was football. Generally playing as a full-back, he missed out on a Blue in the 1920 match,[158] but made up for this with appearances in the Varsity matches of December 1921, in a 3-0 defeat at Stamford Bridge, and December 1922, in an unexpected 2-0 win at the Crystal Palace. Newspaper reports of his matches during his Cambridge seasons suggest a strong but fallible player, but he saved the best until it really mattered, for *The Times*' report of the 1922 Varsity Match says that 'in all probability [he] never played so well in his life as yesterday'.[159]

Football continued to be an important part of his life after leaving Cambridge, as he played as a defender in 24 matches for the Corinthians over the five seasons starting 1922/23,[160] and also represented Cambridgeshire.

But as his Corinthians link shows, he was always only an amateur sportsman. After leaving the university in 1922, he secured a teaching job at King's School at nearby Ely. Initially he took the job for just a year, but in the end he stayed at King's, teaching games and English, for the whole of his working life, retiring at the end of 1959.

His legacy at the school is profound. In 1924 he introduced a house system for school sports, and later he became housemaster of one of the school's [then] four houses; later still, a new house was named in his honour. As

---

158   He played in the place of one of the regular full-backs in several of the games leading up to the Varsity match, but was replaced by the regular man for the Blues match itself. For the University against Nunhead in November, he turned out alongside four others better known as cricketers: goalkeeper Percy Chapman and forwards Gilbert Ashton, Hubert Ashton and A.G.Doggart.

159   *The Times*, 14 December 1922.

160   See Rob Cavallini, *Play Up Corinth*, Stadia, 2007.

senior games master he was in charge of cricket and football (amongst other sports), set up a badminton club, organised the annual sports day, coached pupils even in his spare time, and was a friend to generations of Eleians. His commitment to the school was shown by his being secretary of the Old Eleians Club from 1933 until 1961, in which year he was the club's president. A further tribute came in 1967 when the school's annual cup for fielding was named the F.W.Wilkinson Cup.

Both within and outside the school, cricket rather than football became, over time, his major sport. In 1924 he made his first appearances for Ely City CC; an end-of-season report remarked that 'it is a pity he cannot play more frequently'. He was able to do so by the 1930s, and was a regular member of the side throughout that decade, his performances peaking in 1935 when he topped both the batting and bowling averages with 476 runs at 39.66 and 51 wickets at 11.68.

He also turned out regularly for sides representing King's School, but his abilities were taking him higher. He first appeared for Cambridgeshire in the Minor Counties competition in a single match in 1923, and was a regular in the side from 1929 until just before the Second World War, captaining them for three seasons from 1935. As at Ely, he played as an all-rounder, generally opening the batting or going in at No.3, and bowling as first change or later. To judge from newspaper reports his batting style is best described as 'patient and steady', though he could certainly hit out when needed. As for his bowling: well, the *Who's Who of Cricketers* calls him a leg-spinner, and although he certainly bowled some deliveries in this style, I am not sure that it describes him fully. Reports that I have read talk of him bowling 'a mixture', and include references to him 'bowling with great fire', 'making the ball swing late', and 'coming off the pitch with a zip': not all terms that one associates with an out-and-out leg-spinner.

Whatever his style, he took nearly 200 wickets in the Minor Counties competition for Cambridgeshire between 1923 and 1946, with best innings figures of six for 13 against Lincolnshire at Boston in July 1932, and a match best of 11 for 112 (six for 69 and five for 43) against Bedfordshire at Bedford School exactly two years later. His 1,700-odd runs include one century, a score of 103 against reigning Minor Counties champions Leicestershire II at Fenner's in August 1932. He reached the 90s on two other occasions.

His century at Fenner's was described in the local press as 'a patient and valuable contribution and something in the nature of an endurance test in the hot sunshine': whether the endurance test was for the batsman or the spectators is not clear! It came during a purple patch in his batting, for between June and August 1932 he hit four centuries in all cricket, comprising scores of 123* and 127 for King's School against Chatteris Town and his own club Ely City respectively, followed by his 103 for the county, which was followed in turn by 103* for Ely City against St Giles. Although he had no comparable purple patch in his bowling, mention should be made of his feat of taking five wickets in six balls for Ely City against Old Lennensians in 1936, in a somewhat brief innings in which one

*Ely City eleven of 1936, in F.W.Wilkinson's thirteenth season with the club.
Standing (l to r): E.B.Oakey, F.Morton, T.W.J.Mott, J.C.Rains,
S.H.Porter, W.G.Eagle, F.Roberson.
Seated: P.L.J.Oakey, F.W.Wilkinson, C.C.Broker, P.S.Morton, J.Tannahill.
On the ground: R.C.Blackwell, R.H.Morton. Four of Wilkinson's colleagues
played for Cambridgeshire at one time or another.*

*F.W.Wilkinson, seated far right, with the King's School, Ely eleven of 1949.
The side won six of its seventeen matches.*

of his team-mates also took four wickets in four balls.

By the later 1930s his very best years were behind him, and from 1939 he was no longer an automatic choice in his county side. His 1938 figures for Cambridgeshire were his poorest yet; he scored only 194 runs at 24.25, and took 12 wickets at 41.66. (It may be worth bearing these figures in mind when considering the issue that forms the next part of this chapter, for these were his last Minor Counties performances before the match at Oxford that is referred to at length below.) He played only five matches for the county in 1939, but returned as a 50-year-old for three more in 1946, at which point his Minor Counties career came to an end, though he was still good enough to appear in a friendly match for Cambridgeshire against Huntingdonshire in 1952 when approaching his 56th birthday.

His active cricket career over, he could now devote himself full-time to his beloved school and its local community. On top of his scholarly and sporting commitments, for a time he was also a member of Ely Urban District Council, as well as being president of the local branch of the Royal British Legion and a member of the local amateur dramatics society.

F.W.Wilkinson died at his home in the city on 26 October 1987, three weeks after his 92nd birthday, leaving a not insubstantial financial inheritance to his second wife, Phyllis, who he had married in 1954 around a year after the death of his first wife Hilda, with whom he had had a daughter and a son. The fine impression he had created locally through his long life is demonstrated by the fact that his death was, literally, front-page news in the *Ely Standard*, where his life was summarised succinctly in these words: 'Outstanding sportsman, beloved teacher and friend, gallant soldier, hard-working member of the community and family man'.

Francis William Wilkinson was certainly all of these. But was he also a first-class cricketer who took a wicket with his first delivery at that level?

I bring you a mystery ...

Let's go back to June 1939. As had been the case since 1933, one of the season's first-class fixtures was a match between a representative Minor Counties side and Oxford University in The Parks. In 1939, this fixture was scheduled to begin on 7 June.

Look at the scorecard in *First-Class Cricket: A Complete Record 1939*,[161] and there is F.W.Wilkinson as a member of the Minor Counties side: a fine reward, you might think, for a long and successful career for Cambridgeshire. Read the notes about the match, and you will see that Wilkinson bowled the first over of the game, and with his very first delivery took the wicket – bowled – of J.M.Lomas.

Look in the *Who's Who of Cricketers*, and you will find his biography: a 15-line entry, longer than that of a bona fide Test player on the opposite page, C.A.Wiles, and longer than those of many other players with far more than a single first-class appearance. This biography tells us that, in

---

161   Jim Ledbetter with Peter Wynne-Thomas: *First-Class Cricket: A Complete Record 1939* , Breedon Books, 1991.

his game against the University, Wilkinson was forced to retire injured after bowling eight overs,[162] and took no further part in the match. In his place, a substitute – D.J.F.Watson, who was an Oxford undergraduate rather than a Minor Counties player – was allowed to bat. So it would appear that F.W.'s entire first-class career consisted of a 'did not bat' and bowling figures of 9-1-24-1.[163] The overs, incidentally, were of eight balls.

But now let's look at some other sources.

In the *Wisden Book of Cricket Records*, there is no mention of F.W. in the list of those taking a wicket with their first ball in first-class cricket. Surprising, but some inadvertent omissions are surely inevitable in a 700-page book of this nature.

But there is also no mention of Wilkinson's first-ball achievement in the brief match report in *Wisden* which, because of his substitution, doesn't even list him in the Minor Counties' team, although it does mention his early injury.

And there is no mention of this achievement in contemporary reports of the match in *The Cricketer*, or in the major broadsheets. Surely a player taking a wicket with his first ball, and then leaving the game through injury, would deserve a mention, especially if this were his first-ever first-class match?

So look instead at some other contemporary newspapers – the *Oxford Mail* for example:

> It is rare that the first ball of a match takes a wicket, but this happened in the Parks this morning in the match between Oxford University and the Minor Counties, when Lomas had the unlucky experience against Wilkinson, of the Yorkshire Second XI ... .[164]

Hang on – what's this about Yorkshire? Surely Wilkinson was a Cambridgeshire man, even if he was born close to a Yorkshire border?

Now look back into the papers for a few days earlier. On 2 June, *The Times* and various other newspapers reported the teams selected by the Minor Counties Cricket Association for the match at Oxford, and for their following match against the West Indies. Both included 'Wilkinson (Yorkshire)', but no Wilkinson from Cambridgeshire. On the day the match at Oxford began, *The Times* even went as far as identifying the player as 'Wilkinson (F.) (Yorkshire)'.

The plot, as they say, thickens. So have another look at the *Who's Who*, and there, immediately below the entry for F.W.Wilkinson is one for 'Wilkinson, Frank', a Hull-based professional;[165] a medium-fast bowler who played 14 first-class matches for Yorkshire between 1937 and 1939. Have some wires got crossed here?

---

162   sic; but Wilkinson actually bowled nine overs in the innings
163   We learn from the *Oxford Mail* that the 24 runs he conceded included a six and a four hit by R.B.Proud off successive deliveries.
164   *Oxford Mail*, 7 June 1939.
165   He actually played his first first-class match, in 1937, as an amateur, and turned professional at the start of the following season.

My first thought, on seeing the report in the *Oxford Mail* early on in my researches into F.W., was that the reporter, having heard of the Yorkshire Wilkinson but not of his Cambridgeshire namesake, had simply assumed, wrongly, that the player in The Parks was the Yorkshireman. However, discovery of the team-list in the earlier papers introduced a much stronger element of doubt. Surely the MCCA, when they announced their team to play at Oxford, knew which Wilkinson they were selecting?

So we look into this a bit deeper, and find what may well be the origin of the confusion in, of all places, a pair of articles in *The Cricket Statistician* in the early 1980s. First, in issue 32 (December 1980), in a short piece entitled 'Duties of a twelfth man', the writer John S.Milner refers to a 'Wilkinson' being substituted in the 1939 match, and continues:

> The Wilkinson involved could have been F.W.Wilkinson of Cambridgeshire, or F.Wilkinson, a successful bowler for Yorkshire II ... I would welcome positive evidence as to his identity.

Ten months later, in issue 35, Robert Brooke includes a list of 'Substitutes batting or bowling' in first-class cricket. He prefaces the list by referring back to Milner's piece, and remarks of the list that 'although we do not claim completeness, it is felt that the following is more comprehensive than has ever appeared before'. The 58th of the 62 entries in Brooke's list concerns the 1939 match, and records that D.J.F.Watson substituted for F.W.Wilkinson. No equivocation here over 'Which Wilkinson?', and from then on, all ACS and ACS-related publications, including the guide to Cambridgeshire cricketers, have credited F.W. with this single first-class appearance.

Frank Wilkinson, of Yorkshire.

So the inevitable question: What 'positive evidence' was adduced between the two articles in *The Cricket Statistician,* sufficient to satisfy its then editor that the wicket-taker in The Parks was F.W., rather than Frank, Wilkinson? I posed this question to Robert Brooke in April 2010, and in his reply he mentioned that he no longer has most of his books, but 'relying on memory I feel it likely that it was F.Wilkinson of Yorkshire, but unsupported memory is not something I usually give much credence to.' I posed the same question to Philip Bailey and Peter Wynne-Thomas, two of the compilers of the *Who's Who,* but neither could offer an unequivocal answer. Philip responded in these terms: 'I have a vague recollection of the MCCA saying it was the Cambridgeshire man, but ... I might have imagined [this] and it would have been Philip Thorn who would have done the player research in most cases.'

Sadly, Philip Thorn, the third compiler of the *Who's Who,* and his vast archive are no longer with us to explore that avenue further. My own approaches to the MCCA have not produced anything more helpful either.

So the question of 'Which Wilkinson?' remains without a definitive answer. Until that answer appears, if it ever does, we cannot be certain whether the name of F.W.Wilkinson should be added to the list on page 93. At this distance, the only evidence we can acquire will surely only be circumstantial.

So let's summarise that evidence.

For the player in The Parks being Cambridgeshire's F.W.Wilkinson, we have the following points:

- on unknown evidence (if any), the ACS and its many publications, and those deriving from them, have identified the player as F.W.
- although he had not previously played for any teams more senior than Cambridgeshire, later in 1939 F.W. was a member of the MCC side that played a non-first-class match against Ireland at Lord's.[166] Was his selection for this game perhaps some form of compensation for his truncated first-class career?
- he has an obituary in the *Wisden* of 1988, page 1216, that refers to him as a first-class player. Whether this was written by someone using ACS-derived sources, or independent sources, we do not know.

Against it being F.W.Wilkinson are these points:

- the 'Wilkinson' in this game is not noted in any contemporary source, nor in any later book of cricket records, as having taken a wicket with his first ball in first-class cricket. In the two other British instances that I have investigated – see the second part of this chapter – the fact that the bowlers concerned took a wicket with their first deliveries in first-class cricket was seized upon, and given prominent coverage
- F.W. was heading for his 44th birthday at the time of the 1939 match, and was allegedly a leg-spinner who was no longer taking large numbers of wickets for Cambridgeshire. Was it likely that such a player would have been asked to bowl the first over of the match in The Parks?
- his performances for Cambridgeshire in 1938, especially as a bowler, had been noticeably less successful than in previous years. In these circumstances, would he really have been a candidate for inclusion in a representative Minor Counties side early in 1939?
- there is no mention in any obituary of F.W. that I have seen, apart from that in *Wisden*, nor in any of the information about him supplied by King's School, of his having had a career, even a very brief one, in first-class cricket.
- moreover, if it had been F.W. who played in The Parks, surely the brevity of his first-class career would have been a novelty that would have earned a particular mention in his more general obituaries. But it doesn't.

---

166   He batted at three in both MCC innings, scoring 25 and 3; the opening pair were E.W.Swanton and the aforementioned J.M.Lomas. Although MCC used seven bowlers in the match, Wilkinson was not one of them.

- as an amateur, F.W. would have been listed as 'F.W.Wilkinson' in any team lists, not, as was the actual case, as 'Wilkinson (F.)'
- MCCA's public announcement of the team for the Oxford match was clear that they had selected the Yorkshireman. Despite Philip Bailey's 'vague recollection' of the MCCA telling him something different, surely their announcement five days before the start of the game is more persuasive than any different statement that they may, or may not, have made several decades later
- there is no mention of F.W.'s selection for the Minor Counties team, nor of any injury incurred by him during that match, in the generally thorough cricket coverage of his local newspaper, the *Ely Standard*.

For the player in The Parks being Yorkshire's Frank Wilkinson, we have the following points:

- the player listed in advance to take part in the match was 'Wilkinson (F.) (Yorkshire)', which not only identifies him as the Yorkshire II player but also correctly identifies him as a professional, which F.W. was not
- a number of contemporary newspapers, and not just those in Yorkshire, refer to the Wilkinson in The Parks as a Yorkshire player
- as might be expected, the *Yorkshire Post* picked up on the selection of a 'local boy': its report on 2 June 1939 of the teams announced by the MCCA is headed 'Yorkshire Colt in Minor Counties Elevens'. And its report of the match on 8 June says that 'Wilkinson, the Yorkshire Colt in the Minor Counties' side, was injured and will play no further part in the match.' Surely this paper, of all papers, would have got such facts right?
- Frank Wilkinson was an opening bowler, so it would not be surprising for him to have been given the first over in The Parks
- Frank Wilkinson missed only one match for Yorkshire II all season – the game against Staffordshire at Stafford on 14 and 15 June. This absence is consistent with him picking up a significant injury on the first day of the game in The Parks.[167]

Against it being Frank Wilkinson are these points:

- his possible claim to an appearance in the game at The Parks was evidently rejected by the editor of *The Cricket Statistician* in 1981, and by compilers of all subsequent ACS-derived publications. The evidence for this rejection is not known
- there is no reference in any of the very brief biographies of Frank Wilkinson that I have seen to him playing a first-class match in 1939 for a team other than Yorkshire.

... and a possible solution

For me, the weight of the circumstantial evidence is persuasive that the

---

167   By contrast, F.W.Wilkinson was back playing on the day after the game at Oxford (10 June), when he scored 67 and took one for 23 for King's School against Ely City.

player in The Parks in June 1939 was Frank Wilkinson of Yorkshire, and not Francis W.Wilkinson of Cambridgeshire. If that view is accepted, F.W. is not entitled to an entry in the list of those taking a wicket with the first ball of their only first-class matches; indeed, sadly he is not entitled to the status of a first-class cricketer at all. And if this view is maintained, Frank Wilkinson is entitled to a revised career record of 15 first-class matches rather than 14, with 27 wickets for 614 runs at an average 22.74, rather than 26 wickets for 590 at an average 22.69, as credited in the *Who's Who of Cricketers*.

The definitive evidence that would resolve this issue one way or the other is still lacking, and, like John Milner 31 years ago, I too would welcome that evidence coming forward. In the meantime, I have reluctantly concluded that F.W.Wilkinson does not strictly qualify as a 'Brief Candle', even though the mystery of his first-class career, if any, is surely worth the telling here.

So the number of first-class cricketers goes down by one; or does it? For I have a candidate - linked to F.W.Wilkinson by the common issue of substitution - for an additional player to be accorded recognition as a first-class player, even though he has not hitherto been granted that status. Again the evidence is only circumstantial, but I am persuaded by it - and the leading expert on the county concerned has not sought to disagree on the matter. The player concerned is one George Edward Tyler, who may or may not have been a full substitute for Warwickshire in their Bank Holiday match against Worcestershire at Edgbaston in August 1919 - a match whose first-class status is itself still questioned in some quarters. But this is not the place to go further into this. The full story must await a further publication ... .[168]

* * * * *

With Wilkinson excluded, there are just two British bowlers in the list of those taking a wicket with their first ball in their only first-class matches. Attempts to establish anything approaching full biographies of them - or even details of exactly how they took their wickets - have, sadly, borne little fruit. I summarise below what I have managed to find out about them so far, and would, of course, welcome any further light that readers of this book may be able to throw upon them.

The man from Briton Ferry

First to join the list was John Johns, universally and understandably known as **Jack Johns**. He was a right-arm fast-medium bowler from the Briton Ferry club in South Wales, where he played alongside his older brother Tom (T.S.) Johns. Jack was born in Briton Ferry on 15 October 1885 and lived there all his life; although he died in Neath General Hospital, his home address was still in Briton Ferry.

---

168   I am currently preparing another book that will cover this point in more detail. I have run a draft of the relevant chapter past Warwickshire expert Robert Brooke, and he has not taken any issue over my conclusions regarding G.E.Tyler.

Jack first played for a county eleven in August 1904 at the age of 18, when he turned out for Players of Glamorgan against the Gentlemen of the county. Opening the batting (not a position he would remotely challenge for later in his career) he scored 22 and, surprisingly in light of later events, did not bowl.

Then all is silent for 16 years. Throughout this period Glamorgan participated in the Minor Counties championship, but it was not until their final year in that competition, 1920, that Jack made his debut at this level. Even then it was in only a single game, against Devon at Neath in July, in which he made a pair and returned figures of 4-0-16-0 in the only innings in which he bowled. Not exactly an eye-catching performance.

Unsurprisingly he did not play for Glamorgan in their first season of first-class cricket in 1921, when they started well but soon fell away as the pressure told on an ageing team. 1922 was no better. For these first two years Glamorgan never had anything approaching a settled side: in 1921 they used 29 players in 18 Championship matches, and in 1922, 38 in 22, twelve of whom played only a single game. One of these dozen players was Jack Johns, called into the game against Somerset at Cardiff Arms Park beginning on 15 July to replace the long-serving but out-of-form bowler Jack Nash. By now Johns was three months short of his 37th birthday, but this was still only a little older than the side's average age, despite the inclusion of two players yet to reach the age of 25. Among his other team-mates were Harry Creber, aged 50, Stamford Hacker, aged 45, and three others aged between 38 and 41.

Rain interruptions marred the first day of the game, and turned what started as a good wicket into one that was 'exceedingly tricky', according to the *Western Mail*. Glamorgan were bowled out for 99 soon after tea, Johns making 1* at No.9. He was then entrusted with the first over of Somerset's reply, and with his first ball dismissed Sydney Rippon to what the *Western Mail* called a 'wonderfully smart piece of stumping' by Norman Riches – not a specialist keeper by any means, though rather more than just an occasional one.[169] What Riches was doing standing up to the first ball of the innings, bowled by an unknown bowler on an uncertain pitch, we can only guess; and because contemporary newspapers are silent on the subject, we can only guess too as to the exact nature of the dismissal. Glamorgan expert Andrew Hignell has suggested to me, plausibly, that Johns began with an off-cutter to the right-handed Rippon, and his first delivery gave Riches the opportunity for a fine leg-side stumping. But there is no contemporary source than can confirm that this was indeed the way the wicket fell.

In his fourth over Johns took another wicket when he bowled Jack MacBryan, also for a duck. His opening spell was described by the *Western Mail* as 'admirable', but this was his last first-class wicket. Somerset struggled on to 77 all out with Johns returning a respectable 11-3-29-2, and then dismissed Glamorgan for 139 – at one stage they were 17 for five.

169   Only B.N.Khanna (Northern India 1927/28) can also claim a stumping dismissal off the first ball he ever bowled in first-class cricket. In Khanna's case, it was the *only* ball he bowled in first-class cricket.

Johns was run out for 3. Somerset got the 162 needed for victory before the end of the second day for the loss of only one wicket, Rippon making up for his first innings failure by scoring a rapid 102*. Johns was one of the victims of his hitting, with an analysis of 7-0-33-0.

He had not done enough to keep his place. The rested and doubtless refreshed 48-year-old Nash regained his spot for the game against Lancashire at Swansea the following week, and Jack Johns disappeared from the county scene. In a season of ever-changing faces in the county side, this was perhaps a harsh rejection for one who had started so well.

Of Jack Johns the man, we know little. From the 1911 census we learn that he worked in the tinplate industry that flourished in South Wales at this time. When he died on 10 January 1956, not long after his 70th birthday, he left a widow, Florence. And that's about it, I fear.

Family portrait of the Johns family, with Jack standing second from the left, taken in about 1903.

Of Jack Johns the bowler, we know rather more, thanks to this description from a local club history, written nearly 60 years after Johns' most famous game, and showing that his memory remained long after the man himself had passed on:

> This more reticent member of the family [i.e. more so than his very unreticent brother Tom] was amongst the very best swing bowlers that have ever represented Briton Ferry cricket. Not tall, nor of powerful frame, Jack Johns brought a solid right arm over in a curve that was the geometrician's delight and, consequently, moved the ball in or away from the bat. His pace was brisk, rising to fast, and when he succeeded in straightening his delivery off the pitch, he was all nigh un-playable ... [he was] a craftsman with

that extra, undefinable 'something' that makes the good player a great one.[170]

Sadly, not good enough – still less, great enough – to secure more than a single first-class appearance, despite the success of his first delivery.

One wicket, many goals

The only other Briton to emulate Johns' feat was also christened John but known as Jack; and his moment of cricketing glory also came at Cardiff. But **Jack Lee** was far better known in sporting circles, though not as a cricketer but as an outstanding bustling football centre-forward.

Born at Sileby north of Leicester, on 4 November 1920, Lee began his football career with local side Quorn Methodists, from where he joined Leicester City during the Second World War. He was nearly 26 when he made his League debut for them, in the Second Division, in 1946/47, but he made his mark early with 18 goals in 24 appearances in that first season.

Jack Lee, of Leicester City F.C.

He had already been 'noticed'. Early in the following season there were rumours of possible moves into the First Division with Derby County or Stoke City. But he stayed with his local club for a further three seasons, scoring in all 84 goals in 137 League and Cup appearances; even today this puts him in the top ten of Leicester City's all-time goalscorers. The highlight during this time was his appearance in the 1948/49 Cup Final, en route to which Leicester had beaten five teams above them in the League, including eventual League champions Portsmouth in the semi-final, before succumbing to a disappointing 3-1 defeat by Wolves at Wembley. In the fifth round Leicester had needed ten goals to get past Luton Town, winning a replay 5-3 after drawing 5-5, with Lee scoring four, at Kenilworth Road.

In the close season of 1950 Lee finally moved into the top division with Derby, for a transfer fee of £18,500. 28 goals in his first season, including four in a 6-5 win over Sunderland, earned him an England call-up. He was selected ahead of Stan Mortensen (dropped) in the team to play Northern Ireland at Windsor Park on 7 October 1950, in a fair old forward line that read Stanley Matthews, Wilf Mannion, Jack Lee, Eddie Baily and Tom Finney. Midway through the second half Lee headed the second goal in England's 4-1 win; but Jackie Milburn replaced him for the next international, and he was not selected again.[171]

---

170   D.H.James, *The Town: One Hundred Years of Briton Ferry Town and Other Cricketers*, Briton Ferry CC, 1981.

171   Lee is therefore one of around 40 footballers – only nine of them post-war, including such names as Bill Nicholson, Tony Kay, Danny Wallace, Francis Jeffers and, most recently, David Nugent – who have scored a goal on their only full international appearance for England.

He stayed with Derby for three more years, where long-time County follower Gerald Mortimer remembers him as 'a graceful mover with a strong shot, but in my mental image I don't see him as a great header of the ball.'[172] But as time went on, knee injuries were reducing his effectiveness. Derby were relegated to Division Two for 1953/54, and at the end of that season Lee moved down one further rung to join Coventry City in Division Three (South). Sadly his cartilage troubles soon got the better of him, and during 1955 he was forced to retire from the game.

He moved in rather less distinguished circles in his cricket career. The *Who's Who of Cricketers* calls him a lower-order right-handed batsman and a right-arm medium-pace bowler; but although his claim to cricketing fame came as a bowler, in practice he seems to have had more ability as a batsman.

The first we hear of him as a cricketer was when he played a couple of matches for Leicestershire Club and Ground [C&G] in the midsummer of 1947. He did not bat in a game that the C&G won by ten wickets, and scored 13 as an opener in the other game; he bowled only a single over in these two matches, as the sixth bowler used by his captain. In the following summer his eight C&G games brought him scores that included 81*, 75*, 48 and 41, all as opener or at three; but he bowled in only one of these eight matches. His last two recorded appearances for the C&G were in June 1950, when he again opened both times, scoring 48 and 51, and bowled in only one game. In the 12 C&G matches in which he is known to have played, he scored 395 runs at 43.88, but bowled a total of only 13 overs, though he did take three wickets in the process.

He had played only the two C&G games in 1947 when he was unexpectedly selected in Leicestershire's first eleven to play Glamorgan at the Arms Park in July 1947. Batsman-who-bowled Frank Prentice had to miss the game for business reasons, and Lee was perhaps seen as something of a like-for-like replacement.

The selection of the local centre-forward was noted in the local papers, but at this time Lee had played only a single season of League football, and was not the bigger star that he later became. In reporting his selection the *Leicester Evening Mail* described him as 'a useful batsman and excellent fielder, who learned his cricket with Quorn in the North Leicestershire League', while the *Leicester Mercury* said that he was 'regarded as a promising batsman and quite a useful fast-medium change bowler [who] has been under the wing of Emmott Robinson, the county coach, who is greatly impressed by his potentialities.'[173]

Cardiff was rainy for the match on 9, 10 and 11 July. Put in to bat, Leicestershire made 175, with Lee scoring three at No.8 – a much lower position than that usually occupied by Frank Prentice – and by the end of the first day Glamorgan's reply had reached 77 for seven. Considering how little he had bowled in his earlier C&G games, it must have been something of a surprise when Lee was asked to bowl the second over of the innings;

---

172   In an e-mail to the writer dated 26 September 2010.
173   *Leicester Evening Mail* and *Leicester Mercury*, 8 July 1947.

and no less of one when he had Arnold Dyson caught close in by Les Berry with his very first delivery. Sadly, there are no reports that tell us any more about the dismissal than this. After a four-over spell (4-0-13-1), Lee was taken off, and over the rest of the first day and the start of the second Jack Walsh, with seven for 53, saw off Glamorgan for 142. Johnnie Clay's seven for 32, including a spell of six for 5 in 11 overs, restricted Leicestershire's second innings to 123. Lee, again at No.8, was bowled by Clay for a duck. But the bad weather that had plagued the game meant that the home side had less than an hour to score the 157 needed for victory, and the game ended as a tame draw. Jack Lee was not called on to bowl any of the 13 overs of Glamorgan's second innings.

Unlike Jack Johns, Jack Lee was due to have a further chance at first-class level. He was selected for the county's next game, at home to Middlesex, but in the end he had to turn the match down following a 'precurrence' of the problems that were to blight his later football career: 'The Leicester City centre-forward had been chosen to play, but was troubled with an old knee injury and had to cry off'.[174]

And despite his success with the bat in later Club and Ground matches, he never played for the county side again, not even for the Second Eleven, and he was never taken on to the county staff. Maybe the need to protect his knee for the football season had something to do with this; but for whatever reason, a potentially promising cricket career had come to a premature end.

I'm afraid I don't know how he spent his first ten years or so after retiring from football, but with a wife, Beryl, and four children, domestic duties were no doubt not insignificant. In the mid-1960s he became the groundsman at Lawrence Sheriff School at Rugby, where he stayed until his retirement in 1984. He seems to have kept his sporting history largely to himself, for as the *Rugby Advertiser* later wrote, 'after 18 years of preparing pitches for others, not many people knew of Jack's own distinguished sporting record'.[175] Instead he dedicated himself to his duties at the school, and 'always ensured cricketers could take pride in the quality of the [school's] square'. Taken with the fact that he spent 18 years at a school whose principal winter sport was rugby rather than soccer, can we read into this that for him, as for some other 'other-sportsmen' in this book, cricket held first place in his affections?

Jack Lee's disappearance into the world of groundsmanship, and his evident modesty about his past achievements, seems to fit with other memories of him. Gerald Mortimer recalls being told that he was 'quiet and self-contained'; and he was, too, a man who never strayed far from home.

Lee never received an obituary in *Wisden*, and his relative obscurity to cricket followers is shown by the fact that his exact date of death is not recorded in CricketArchive. In fact he died on 12 January 1995 at St Cross Hospital in Rugby, a couple of months after his 74th birthday.

---

174   *Leicester Mercury*, 12 July 1947.
175   *Rugby Advertiser*, 19 January 1995.

His cremation was held at Loughborough, back 'home' in Leicestershire. A local football follower wrote to the *Leicester Mercury* to describe him as 'a great sportsman ... wonderful value for his £15 a week'.[176]

Which is how we should remember a fine footballer and a man who, had things turned out differently, might have proved a useful county cricketer.

---

176   Letter from Alf Wilson in the *Leicester Mercury*, 21 January 1995.

Chapter Seven

A Life in Cricket

For the players whose lives in cricket have been recorded in the preceding pages, cricket was never a full-time career. None was ever taken on to a county's staff, or played as a pro in a League team. The majority were amateurs for whom cricket was only a diversion in lives that led them down much more varied paths.

But it is appropriate that we should end with a man for whom cricket has been a dominant factor affecting his whole life, and for whom for many years it was his career as well as a diversion. Like all the others in this book, **Bob Richards** played only a single first-class match; on the face of it the high point of a playing career[177] that began in his early teens and continues today when he is nearer to 80 years of age than to 70, though you'd never believe that to see or talk to him. But when a few years after this game the opportunity unexpectedly arose to make cricket his profession, then, fittingly for a wicketkeeper, he seized it with both hands, and it remained his livelihood until retirement. Truly Bob's has been, and continues to be, a 'life in cricket'.

Yet you wouldn't have predicted that from his beginnings. Born into an RAF family at Winchester on 5 August 1934 and with no family background in sport, Bob must be one of very few first-class cricketers to get into the game via, of all things, baseball. His family had no particular Hampshire connections; he says that his parents must have just stopped off there for a few weeks on one of his father's postings. His early years were mostly spent at Pitsea in Essex,[178] but between the ages of nine and eleven Bob lived in Canada, where his father was posted during the War. The family was fortunate to survive the Atlantic crossing; the sister ship to the one they were on was sunk. Through playing a little baseball, Bob discovered that he had one special skill; he could catch pretty much anything that was thrown at him. So when he returned to Pitsea after the War, knowing next to nothing of either cricket or football, his catching ability meant that at school he was placed in goal in the soccer side, and in the slips in the cricket team.

Bob's wicketkeeping career began at Craylands County Secondary School in Basildon, at the age of 13, purely by chance. During a practice session on the outfield a couple of days before a school match, he bowled a ball that reared up and hit the regular keeper on the nose, putting him out of action. So, because he could catch, Bob took over the gloves: and he has never relinquished them from that day on.

---

177   But only on the face of it: see pages 111 and 112.
178   Pitsea was then a village quite separate from the later New Town of Basildon, with which it has now merged.

The cricket bug had bitten. On leaving school he and some of his school team-mates played together for Bowers Boys Club against local village sides. Despite their youth – most were aged 15 or 16 – they rarely lost, because they had some very strong players who went on to become regulars at leading local club sides, and at least one of whom (apart from Bob) briefly attracted the interest of Essex C.C.C. From there, it was on to playing for Pitsea St Michael's, before Bob decided to follow his father into the RAF.

He spent three years in uniform – much of it, it seems, in an all-white uniform. His Services cricket, which included playing for RAF Middle East and for a Combined Services team on tour in Malta, was played with and against some very good players, including National Servicemen, and Bob says that playing a couple of years of cricket of this standard was 'a huge experience'.[179]

And a decisive one too. With increased confidence in his abilities, when Bob left the RAF at the age of 21 he decided to follow his erstwhile team-mate and life-long friend Ken Sandeman, the former wicketkeeper whose face he had damaged with his bowling a few years previously, by joining Westcliff-on-Sea Cricket Club. This was Trevor Bailey's club, and the strongest side in the area.

Within three weeks, Bob had graduated through Westcliff's third and second teams to their first eleven: he retained that berth for the next 30-odd years. Selection for games for the Club Cricket Conference followed, in the first of which Bob volunteered to open the batting following a request from the captain ('a jolly nice chap with a cravat', as Bob recalls, with rather more than a hint of sarcasm) and promptly added 180-odd with David Evans, a Hertfordshire Minor Counties player and future right-wing MP and controversial chairman of Luton Town F.C.

At much the same time – the mid-1960s – Bob was coming to the notice of the Essex club, and playing games for the seconds and for the Club and Ground eleven. He made his debut in the Second Eleven competition in a single match in 1966, and for the next three seasons – following the mid-season departure from the club of Rodney Cass – was first-choice keeper for the seconds when available. He had to fit his playing – for the Club Cricket Conference and Essex Cricket Association, as well as for the county side – around his day job in the accounts department of Marconi Ltd at Basildon, initially 'fiddling time off' when he could: 'a day sick here and there'. But as time went on, the Essex keeper and captain Brian 'Tonker' Taylor came to see Bob as his natural reserve, and wrote to Marconi requesting extra holiday for him. Fortunately the personnel officer was 'cricket mad, absolutely barmy for cricket, and when he got a letter from Brian Taylor he was over the moon.' So Bob got a few more days' holiday as a result.

Tonker Taylor was renowned for his durability. Between 1961 and 1972 he played in 301 consecutive Championship matches, and during much of

---

179   Throughout this chapter, unattributed quotations are taken from my interview with Bob on 13 July 2010, or from our subsequent correspondence.

this period, Essex did not even bother to engage a second specialist keeper. Thus Bob was never taken on to the county staff, though he recalls that the prospect was floated at one time, but came to nothing because of shortage of funds. So he was particularly proud when he was awarded his second eleven cap in 1969, a rare achievement for a non-staff player. He recalls that Taylor would ring him occasionally, to check that he was keeping himself ready if the call should come: 'Don't forget, if I get crocked, you're in.' But Tonker never did get crocked, or if he did, he never let anyone know about it; and Bob remained purely a second eleven player.[180] He was happy to be so, even turning down an approach to play for Hertfordshire so that he could continue to be available for Essex.

There was one especially bright moment during this period. In 1967 a strong International Cavaliers side were playing a series of 40-over televised Sunday afternoon matches against the counties, a precursor to the John Player League that began in 1969. On 9 July 1967, their fixture was against Essex at Bob's home ground at Westcliff. Godfrey Evans was originally picked to keep wicket for the Cavaliers, but shortly before the game he had to drop out, and Taylor swapped sides to take his place in the Cavaliers XI, alongside the likes of Garry Sobers, Rohan Kanhai, Hylton Ackerman, Jim Laker and Neil Hawke. Taylor invited Bob to take his place in the otherwise full-strength Essex side, and he leapt at the opportunity. Before a 'sun-drenched crowd of 4,500' at Chalkwell Park, as reported by the *Southend Standard*, 425 runs were scored in 80 overs, the Cavaliers winning a tight game by nine runs, scoring 217 for seven to Essex's 208 for eight. Bob made a catch and a stumping, and allowed no byes. The stumping was G.Sobers st Richards b Bailey, but sadly for posterity, the batsman was not Garry Sobers but his older brother Gerry.[181] Later, batting at No.8 for the county side Bob was dismissed by the Ackerman-Laker combination for eight, though in the less likely form of 'ct Laker b Ackerman'. His innings included a clout over mid on for four as he tried to increase the scoring rate – he was conscious that the winners received £100 and he wanted his share – but he was then caught trying to repeat the dose.

For Bob this match was the high point of his playing career. He remembers well his leg-side stumping of Gerry Sobers: 'A very, very fast stumping. As I took the bails off I spun to the umpire, shouting at him for the stumping and I remember the whole crowd went up behind the umpire; everybody jumped just like they'd seen a goal scored.' As a batsman he didn't face Garry Sobers, but he stood behind him while he made 38, playing 'some beautiful shots', and he also recalls Rohan Kanhai playing his crowd-pleasing 'falling over hook shots'.

Home ground, sunny day, big crowd, big names, close finish, and on

180   When pressed, and only when pressed, Bob reckoned that, in his prime, he was a better pure keeper than Taylor, and felt that this view was shared by some players who dropped into the second eleven for the odd game. But of course Taylor had secured the first-eleven berth before Bob arrived on the scene, and at county level had considerably more to offer as a batsman

181   Garry Sobers was also dismissed in this match by Trevor Bailey, his future biographer. Bob recalls that Garry allowed himself to be bowled through the gate, as this was a benefit match for Bailey.

television too. Is it any wonder that this is the game above all that Bob recalls as the highlight of his playing career?

Certainly it was more of a highlight than the disappointing game three years later in which he made his sole first-class appearance. Still playing regularly for Westcliff but with his place in the county seconds now under challenge from, in particular, the future Cambridge Blue Richard Baker, Bob was delighted to be asked by Taylor to keep wicket in the match against the touring Jamaican XI at Leyton starting on 19 August 1970. Taylor also played in this match, but was content to hand the gloves to someone else.

At the time, Bob didn't know that this was a first-class match; he only found out some time later 'when some kind soul [not the present writer!] sent me a sheet of players who played one first-class match and not contributed in any way during the game.' The Essex side had a few newcomers: debuts were given to batsman Vic Brooks and to Keith Pont as well as to Bob. Sadiq Mohammad made his only appearance for the county. Their opponents were pretty much the full-strength Jamaica XI that had recently finished as runners-up in the Shell Shield (Lawrence Rowe, Maurice Foster and all), and who were now undertaking a brief and little-noticed tour of four first-class and five other matches.

Bob's game too was brief and little-noticed. The first two matches of the Leyton Festival[182] had both reached a conclusion, but rain set in on 19 August and no play was possible on the first scheduled day of the Jamaica match. Play began at 2 pm on the following day, when Essex scored 107 for six before declaring at the tea interval. In 'gathering gloom', as *Wisden* puts it, Jamaica scored 116 for three in the remaining hour and three-quarters before close of play. A night of heavy rain followed, and the match was called off at 11 am the following day.

So ended Bob Richards' first-class career, had he but known it. For him, this was 'just another game of cricket'; as already noted, he did not appreciate at the time that it was a first-class match, and of course at the end of it he did not know that he would not play at that level again. Today he has no mementoes of the match, not even a scorecard. Such as it was, it was a pretty quiet game for him. He did not bat in the Essex innings: the team list in *Wisden* has him at No.11, though Bob feels he might have gone in a place or two higher in practice. Although he kept wicket for the 33.5 overs of the Jamaica innings, 8.5 of them bowled by Keith Fletcher (!), he did not get a catch or a stumping; he recalls that no chances were given. Then again, neither did he concede a bye.

Apart from the rain and the consequent small crowd, Bob has one enduring memory of the game. When Jamaica batted, Keith Boyce opened the bowling. Bob had played with him before, and so stood back at his normal distance, and was taking the ball comfortably enough. But 'then he let a rocket go, an absolute Exocet, which lifted off a length, and I want

---

182   Leyton had long since ceased to be the county's headquarters ground, but between 1957 and 1977 it hosted an annual 'festival' of between two and four first-class matches during August each year.

The newly restored pavilion at Leyton, photographed in 2010.
Bob Richards spent the first day of his first-class career here waiting for
play to start against Jamaica in August 1970. Twenty-seven other cricketers
have played their only first-class match at this ground.

to be six or eight yards further back. I managed to jump and get it in the left glove up here and came down with it thinking, "Christ, I got away with that." And then Tonker shouted from mid wicket, "Two hands in this team." He didn't say "well taken" or anything; just "Two hands in this team."' A hard man to please was Tonker.[183]

Bob was 36 years and 76 days old when he made his first-class debut on 20 August. In the twentieth century, only about a dozen players had made their Essex debuts at a greater age. But Essex were now looking to younger men to keep wicket in their second eleven. For most matches in 1970 the role was given to Richard Baker, and in 1971 it was shared between Baker and a 17-year-old named Graham Gooch. Bob was recalled for a single appearance in both 1974 and 1975, but for most of the early 1970s his cricket was for Westcliff and for the Club Cricket Conference. The latter included a prestigious tour to Australia, under the captaincy of the aforementioned David Evans, at the same time that Ray Illingworth was winning the Ashes back for England.

1975 saw a change in Bob's life away from cricket, for after many years with Marconi he moved to work in the accounts department of James Abbott, estate agents in Leigh-on-Sea. Cricket played an important part not so much in the move itself, but in the role that Bob played for his new employer. In his words, 'Initially I applied for, and got, a job as property negotiator [but] then I received a phone call from the company secretary who was also our Westcliff opening bowler, who advised me that my job would entail working on Saturdays (whoops) and that he could offer me a job in the accounts department instead.' It was no contest: cricket won

---

183   Richards is 5ft 6in tall; Taylor was some three inches taller. But would Taylor really have been able to take such a delivery with two hands?

out again.

In 1979, Bob's life took its final cricket-ward turn. By now he had taken the first-level coaching qualification, and was doing some part-time coaching at Ilford Cricket School; but by day he was still working for the estate agents. Then 'a guy in the office who was cricket-mad said: "There's a vacancy in the paper for an assistant coach with Essex County Cricket Club; that's right up your alley. Why don't you apply?"'

Bob had always been interested in the mechanics of sport, and 'what causes what' in the techniques of games. A coaching job would allow him to develop this interest, as well as extending his involvement in cricket.[184] So he applied; and he was duly appointed as assistant coach to Graham Saville. Soon afterwards, Saville secured a job as Eastern Region coach with the National Cricket Association, and Bob became Essex's senior coach, a post he held for 20 years until his retirement aged 65 in 1999.[185] He was not just a coach, either; for many years he also managed the finances and the bookings at the cricket school at Chelmsford, as well as organising future courses. In due course he too became an Eastern Region staff coach, working under Saville.

On the coaching side alone, his responsibilities were considerable. He ran one-to-one coaching sessions through the day and evening for boys (and a few girls) and adults; day courses during the school holidays; evening coaching with county squads of all ages, including all the pros still in the country during the winter months; and pre-season sessions with staff players. It was not a quiet life, especially during the school holidays when the place was 'full of kids'.

As well as securing the qualifications required to coach at this level, including passing an advanced coaching course at Lilleshall in 1979, Bob also has the unusual distinction of holding both a City and Guilds certificate and an NVQ in cricket, testimony to the seriousness and thoroughness with which he undertook his new task after finally joining the Essex staff.

And although Bob's speciality was wicketkeeping, he had to coach all aspects of the game. Neither batting nor bowling were mysteries to him. As a batsman – he bats right-handed – he describes his style as 'nurdling and tucking it away': he is principally a back-foot player who scores mostly square of or behind the wicket off the quicker bowlers because he doesn't have the levers to hit through the ball with great power, though he can slog effectively when the occasion arises. This style has proved successful: he regards himself as a 'batsman/wicketkeeper' at club level, though more of a 'keeper/batsman' at higher levels. He has half a dozen centuries to his name, the best being a score of 123 for Leigh against Ilford, 'and most of the guys I got it against I have coached!'

---

184 Bob himself was never coached, either as keeper or as batsman; he learned his cricket simply by copying, and by instinct.

185 When retirement came, he didn't give up his coaching duties overnight, but on his own initiative he continued working part-time at the cricket school at Chelmsford for a while.

You won't find his name down as a bowler in any scorecards on CricketArchive, but when he became a coach he found himself bowling, slow left-arm, about 300 overs in the nets each week. That sort of experience once stood him in good stead in a match when he was playing against Leigh for a 'Selected XI' for whom the (then new) Essex keeper Neil Smith was behind the stumps. 'We'd got about 230 and we tried all the bowlers. They were chasing our score, and they were going to knock it off easily: we'd only taken one wicket. So the skipper tossed the ball to me: I don't know why, but he did. I bowled what I normally bowl in the nets, trying to keep it up to the bat, and I'd got a guy at short extra cover and they obligingly hit two straight to him. Then Smithy caught one and stumped one, then I bowled a great big long hop which was smacked straight at square leg. ... I ended up with six for 30 and we won the game.' That's what 300 overs a week of practice can do for you.

As a coach, Bob believed in constant encouragement for his charges, but demanded self-discipline from them. He drew his coaching techniques from many sources, and devised specific coaching methods to meet the needs of particular players. As an example, he told me that to help one of his early charges, a nine-year-old Stephen Peters, improve his judgement of length, Bob would bowl as fast as he could, and Peters got a point for every time he judged the length correctly: Bob got a point every time he didn't. 'We played for ten points. It started off about five-each, but then gradually after a few weeks he was beating me ten-nil, all the time. And he never looked back after that.' Bob does not claim special credit for Peters' later success in the game. He says he showed huge natural potential when he first saw him hitting a tennis ball with his father on the boundary at Upminster, and is happy to acknowledge that many other coaches had a hand in his subsequent development; but he certainly contributed helpfully to the development of the skills that led Peters to a century in the final when England won the Under-19 World Cup in 1998, and to a successful career with Essex and later with Northamptonshire and Worcestershire.

All the time Bob was coaching for Essex, he was continuing to play club cricket.[186] He made his last appearance in the Westcliff first eleven at the age of 61 in the mid-1990s. For a couple of seasons before that he had played for Leigh-on-Sea, but Westcliff invited him back to cope with Barbadian quick bowler Hattian Graham, who was due to arrive at the club, courtesy of Trevor Bailey and Keith Boyce. 'So he duly arrived and he was quick but erratic, so I am going all over the place; he was great fun.'

After a while, Bob yielded his place in the Westcliff first team to a youngster whom he had coached, and after a period in the second team he was invited to rejoin Leigh as their first-team keeper for a few seasons. At the same time he 'carried on playing any cricket that was going; for the Forty Club and touring teams, and all sorts.'

Cricket was for a while principally a mid-week activity; but you can't keep

---

186   He also made a final appearance in a non-championship Second Eleven match in 1985, aged nearly 51, in an early-season game against an Essex League XI on his home ground at Westcliff.

Freddie Brown, Ted Dexter, Les Lenham, Bob Richards and others with a group of youngsters at Chelmsford in 1979. Bob is second from left in the back row.

Bob Richards coaching a fellow wicketkeeper at the Chelmsford Indoor Cricket School in the 1970s.

a good man down, and nowadays he's back playing Saturday cricket. After leaving Essex to live in Norfolk in 2007, his Forty Club contacts led to him being invited to play a few end-of-season games for Bradenham, in the hope of helping the side to win the league and gain promotion. A few eyebrows were initially raised at the idea of a 73-year-old wicketkeeper joining the club, but he quickly won over the doubters. His performances for them were described by a team-mate as 'a master-class', and Bob says, 'Of course, they won the games, but not by my efforts, but by theirs. And they won promotion.'

Another Forty Club contact invited him to play Sunday cricket for the Essex club Frinton in 2009, where he played in the Sunday second eleven; for 2010 he was promoted to the Saturday second side. He still enjoys the game and the players, and their beautiful ground at Ashlyns Road, and though nowadays he says, 'I just turn up and play', he is happy to give coaching advice as well, without in any way forcing it on his club-mates.

Since 2007 he has also been playing regularly for the Two Counties Over-50s and Over-60s sides.[187] His continuing skill and speed are well shown by the fact that, in 79 matches to the end of the 2011 season, he had recorded over twice as many stumpings for them (57) as he had taken catches (25).

Bob's wicket-keeping style is unfussy. He likes to stand up to attack with the seamers when it is likely to be helpful to the team, but he does not do so out of bravado. When playing for Westcliff with Trevor Bailey bowling, he would start by standing back when Bailey was coming in off his full county run, but would move up to the stumps once his initial lift and snap had gone: otherwise he wouldn't feel sufficiently under control to take the ball cleanly. He remembers some fine leg-side stumpings off Bailey's bowling, often as a result of some pre-planning between them, after Bailey had been quick to spot some vulnerability in the batsman's method.[188]

One of his proudest claims is that he has dropped only one routine catch standing back since 1971. He dropped a head-high catch in that year and he thought: 'I don't do that. If ever I drop another one, I'll hang up the gloves.' It was 1992 before he had to reconsider that idea, when he put one down in a game 'in September, it was raining, it was pitch dark and the ball was like a lump of soap and it went in and squiggled around and dropped out. And I've never dropped another one since.'

For a cricketer who has been a wicketkeeper for over 60 years, Bob's hands are in remarkably good shape, with no significant bruises or breakages. He is pleased to claim that his hands are in far better condition than Brian Taylor's: 'Tonker's broken every bone he's got!' In part this is of course down to his easy taking of the ball, but it is also helped by wearing exactly the right sort of gloves. He took this aspect of the game very seriously, and for five or six years in the late 1980s he designed wicketkeeping gloves

---

187   The 'Two Counties' are Essex and Suffolk.
188   Bob recalls Trevor Bailey as a good and sociable club member who, when able to turn out for Westcliff, was 'just another team member' who never sought to use his reputation to influence club matches, or the captain, unless asked.

for Slazenger – after first telling the company that he could make a better pair than those they provided for him under a sponsorship deal. This was in the days when keepers' gloves were moving towards the design of a baseball mitt, with substantial webbing between thumb and first finger, and Bob's designs took full advantage of the rather looser regulations that applied at that time. Nothing wrong with that, of course, and Bob's gloves were very highly regarded. But when a new man took over at Slazenger, Bob's services were dispensed with and, as far as he is concerned, their gloves have never been so good since.

Bob Richards at home in Harleston, Norfolk, in 2010.

Not just cricket

For over 60 years, Bob Richards has been an outstanding wicketkeeper at all levels of the game, right up, briefly, to first-class level. It can fairly be said that cricket is his life, though not all of it. He is married and has a daughter who he describes as 'a badminton queen', who has taken a coaching qualification in the sport – like father, like daughter. He says it took his wife Margaret about 30 years to appreciate cricket, though nowadays she analyses the game with the best of them; but she still hasn't got round to liking football.

Bob himself remained a footballer for many years, moving out of goal when his lack of height counted against him – 'an eight-foot crossbar was too much' – and becoming first a winger and then an inside-forward, before finally moving back to play as sweeper. He commented: 'For the first time in my life I'm facing the ball. And once I was facing the ball, it was like reading a map. You could see the play in front of you, you could follow the play, you could move into position, cut the passes off and start your own. It was wonderful, and I thought, "Why haven't I done this years ago?"'

He played football regularly until his mid-40s, turning out for Marconi in the Business Houses League, at a good standard with several ex-pros playing, and also appearing three times for a representative Thurrock League XI, and playing a few games in the reserve side of Basildon United.

Bob's other main sport was table-tennis, where he held his own in the top local leagues. He was never as good as his mate Ken Sandeman, and not quite up to county standard, but still well up there with the best league players in Southend, Thurrock and Basildon. As with cricket, he also took a coaching qualification, passing his exam despite having his right leg in plaster following a football mishap. There's dedication.

A toast to them all

So, surely a life in cricket; but not a life wholly of cricket.

Bob Richards is a man for whom cricket has shaped almost his entire life, from his early schooldays, through his days in the RAF and in non-cricket employment, when bosses and others appear to have stretched the rules a little to allow him to play more, through his 20 years in a tracksuit at Chelmsford, right up to the present when he is still playing regularly, and to a good standard, in his later 70s.

At all levels of the game, he has always given his best. In our meeting, he said more than once that his aim, in every game, was simply to be the best on the day, once adding, 'When I play, I look at the other wicketkeeper and if he has a good game, I think "I'm going to be better than that."' And although the speed of play may vary the higher the standard of the game, for Bob every match is 'just another game': not in the sense of another boring day at the office, far from it, but rather that every game is as special as every other one; they are all opportunities to enjoy and to excel. To Bob, even his one and only first-class match was just another game of cricket rather than being, as you might have thought, the most significant or important game he ever played in.

Ronald Mason lauded Fred Hyland on the grounds that 'the distinction that he can wave in the teeth of all competitors is an indisputable and proud one: he had played first-class cricket; and what proportion of genuine cricket-lovers can say the same?' But six pages later he went on to write: 'The distinction is perhaps one without a difference; in fact it may be entirely illusory, and to those who have once stepped across the magic line there is no glamour at all.'

Bob Richards is, I fear, evidence that Mason was right on the latter point, at least in some cases; but then how much 'glamour' could anyone glean from a dark and rainy three days at Leyton cricket ground in the 1970s? On those three days, Bob did indeed step over the magic line, and I for one look at him differently for that, and with extra respect. But his personal appreciation is of cricket itself, and not the fact that he, just once, made it to the first-class level. In Mason's words, let him 'stand toast' to all those who simply love the game, at whatever level they can achieve; and who play it to the very best of their abilities for as long as they are physically able.

Acknowledgements

Many people have helped in producing this book, but it is right that I begin with my thanks to a few key contributors. First must be David Jeater, for his ever-constructive guidance from the early stages onwards. Equally, I must give profound thanks to Stuart Moffat and Bob Richards for so willingly giving up their time to me, and to Charlie Kuzniar for transcribing my interviews with them.

For their general help, my thanks go in particular to Philip Bailey, for various contributions deriving from the CricketArchive database; to Mike Spurrier, for his assistance on the military careers of some of the Candles; and to Chris Overson, Robby Wilton and Peter Gilbert for their interest and general support (mostly!) throughout the project.

For help on specific individuals I must thank in particular the following: John Boomer, Rita Boswell (Archivist, Harrow School), Robert Brooke, Gerry Byrne, Tony Debenham, Anthony Dougall (Brighton Brunswick CC), Michael Frost (Inner Temple library), Adam C.Green (Trinity College, Cambridge), Eric Greenwood, Andrew Hignell, Neil Jenkinson, Dennis Lambert, Julian Lawton-Smith, Neil Leitch, Malcolm Lorimer, Gerald Mortimer, Dr A.R.Morton (RMA, Sandhurst), Stephen Musk, Roy New, Anne Parkinson (Dick Wooster's daughter), David Pracy, Pauline Raymond (Sedlescombe), Margaret Richards, Michael J.Sampson (Blundell's School), Elizabeth Stazicker (King's School, Ely), Michael Talbot-Butler, Joe Webber, Judith Wilde (Brunner Mond, Northwich), Guy Williams (Wellington College) and Peter Wynne-Thomas. My thanks for their help go too to countless librarians and assistants at the British Library at Colindale, the RAF Museum at Hendon, the National Archives at Kew, the MCC library at Lord's, and at numerous local libraries and record offices across England, and beyond.

My special thanks go too to Gerald Hudd and Chris Overson for their assiduous proof-reading, and to those who have supplied many of the illustrations: Eric Greenwood, Andrew Hignell, Richard Holdridge, Roger Mann, Jonathan and David Noble, David Potter, Bob Richards, Mike Spurrier, Elizabeth Stazicker, Geoff Treasure (Fred Hyland's 'grandson-in-law'), Alan Virgo (Woodvale Cemeteries, Brighton), and the Hampshire and Northamptonshire Record Offices. Other illustrations derive chiefly from my own dubious camera work.

Many other people have earned my gratitude for smaller, though no less valuable, contributions towards the finished article. I apologise to any who look for their names here and don't find them. You have my thanks already, and I am happy to reiterate them more generally here.

It is customary to conclude with an expression of thanks to the author's other half; and I do so unhesitatingly, for without Judith's tolerant support over many months, none of this would have been remotely possible, or as much fun. And yes, she does make a very nice cup of tea.

K.S.W.

Bibliography

The principal sources consulted during the preparation of *Brief Candles*, in addition to those cited in the text, have been the following:

Books

General

Army Register, various years

Philip Bailey, Philip Thorn and Peter Wynne-Thomas, *Who's Who of Cricketers*,
    Hamlyn, 1993

Philip Bailey, Robert Brooke and others (ed), *First Class Cricket Matches*
    for seasons 1801 to 1924, ACS Publications, various years

Rowland Bowen, *Cricket: A History*, Eyre and Spottiswoode, 1970

Robert Brooke, *The Collins Who's Who of English First-Class Cricket 1945-1984*,
    Collins Willow, 1985

Dictionary of National Biography, Oxford University Press, 2004-2011

Kelly's Directories (various)

Jim Ledbetter and others (ed), *First-class Cricket: A Complete Record* for
    seasons 1926 to 1939, ACS Publications and Breedon Books, various years

Frederick Lillywhite's Cricket Scores and Biographies, various years

E.W.Swanton (ed), *Barclay's World of Cricket*, Willow Books, 1986

Who's Who and *Who Was Who*, various dates

Peter Wynne Thomas, *The Complete History of Cricket Tours at Home and Abroad*,
    Hamlyn, 1989

Josiah Coulthurst

East Lancashire Cricket Club, *History and Reminiscences*, 1864-1947,
    East Lancashire CC, 1947

Dave Edmundson, *See the Conquering Hero Comes*, MMLL, 1992

Eric Greenwood, *A History of the East Lancashire Club, Part 1: 1864-1944*
    and associated statistical volume, Red Rose Books, 1999

Alan West, *One Hundred years of the Ribblesdale Cricket League 1892-1992*,
    Cranden Press, 1992

Robert Gregory

Chris Hobson, *Airmen Died in the Great War, 1914-1918*, Hayward, 1995

W.P.Hone, *Cricket in Ireland*, The Kerryman, 1955

Michael Harbottle

Peter Fry, *Dorset 100 Not Out: A Celebration of 100 years of the Dorset County
    Cricket Club, 1896-1996*, The Author, 1996

H.M.Hinde

Tony Percival, *Berkshire Cricketers, 1844-2008*, ACS Publications, 2008

F.J.Hyland

Andrew Hignell, *Rain Stops Play*, Frank Cass, 2002

Emile McMaster

R. Courtenay Welch, *The Harrow School Register, 1800-1911*,
    Longmans Green and Co, 1911

Marylebone Cricket Club, *Matches for the Season 1888*, MCC, 1888

F.W. and Frank Wilkinson

Tony Percival, *Cambridgeshire Cricketers, 1819-2006*, ACS Publications, 2007

Peter Thomas, *Yorkshire Cricketers, 1839-1939*, Derek Hodgson, 1973

Magazines, newspapers and regular publications

Annuals and Periodicals
Cricket: A weekly record of the game, The Cricketer and The Cricketer International, Cricket Quarterly, The Cricket Statistician, Journal of the Cricket Society, The Wisden Cricketer, Wisden Cricketers' Almanack, Wisden Cricket Monthly

Specific articles in other periodicals
Maj Guy Bennett, Berkshire Cricket Memories, in Berkshire Cricket Yearbook 1999
    (reprinted from an unknown earlier source, c.1955)
Ken Coates, European Nuclear Disarmament, in The Spokesman, No.38, 1980
Neil Jenkinson, More of the late Frederick J.Hyland, in Hampshire CCC Yearbook
    2003

National newspapers
The Times, The Manchester Guardian/Guardian, The Daily Telegraph, The Glasgow Herald/Herald, The Independent, The Irish Independent, The Irish Times, The Scotsman, The Sportsman, Sporting Life, The London Gazette; The Cape Argus (Cape Town), The Cape Times (Cape Town), The Daily Independent (Kimberley), The Diamond Fields Advertiser (Kimberley)

Local newspapers
Berkshire Chronicle, Blackburn Times, Blackburn Weekly Telegraph, Bournemouth Echo, Brighton Argus, Brighton Gazette, Camberley News, Cambridge Chronicle, Cambridge Daily News, Cambridge Evening News, Clitheroe Advertiser & Times, Croydon Chronicle, Dorset Daily Echo, Eastbourne Chronicle, Eastbourne Gazette, Ely Standard, Hampshire Advertiser and Independent, Hastings and St Leonards Observer, Isle of Wight County Press, Kettering Leader, Lancashire Evening Telegraph, Leicester Evening Mail, Leicester Mercury, Northampton Daily Chronicle, Northampton Daily Echo, Northampton Mercury, Northern Daily Telegraph, Northwich Guardian, Norwood News, Norwood Press and Dulwich Advertiser, Oxford Mail, Oxford Times, Rugby Advertiser, South London Mail, Southend Standard, Southern Daily Echo, Southland Times (New Zealand), Sussex Daily News, Sussex Express, Sutton Advertiser, Waltham Forest Guardian and Gazette, Western Daily Press, Western Mail, Wiltshire Times, Yorkshire Post

Websites
www.ancestry.com, www.british-genealogy.com, www.cricketarchive.com, www.cricketeurope4.net, www.cricketscotland.com, www.cricinfo.com, www.cwgc.org, www.eastsussexinfigures.org.uk, www.england.11v11.com, www.ercrugby.com, www.escis.org.uk, www.findmypast.co.uk, www.historyireland.com, www.innertemple.org.uk, www.irishnewsarchive.com, www.lancashireleague.com, www.newsuk.co.uk, www.oldeleans.org.uk, www.richthofen.com, www.twgpp.org, www.visionofbritain.org.uk, http://en.wikipedia.org, www.winningtonpark.co.uk, www.1914-18.net

Unpublished materials
Berkshire CCC archive records
Hampshire CCC scorebooks and archive records
Harrow School Roll of Honour
David J.Lane, Fallen Wickets and Far-Flung Memories: A Brief History of Dorset
    County Cricket, 1776 to 1974, unpublished MS.
Northamptonshire CCC scorebooks
Oxford University records
Oxfordshire CCC scorebooks
Tony Percival, Dorset Cricketers, unpublished MS for ACS

Appendix
Some Statistics

Career records in Minor Counties and Second Eleven competitions

			M	I	NO	R	HS	Ave	100/50
J.Coulthurst	Lancs II	1921-22	6	9	4	74	38	14.80	-
M.N.Harbottle	Dorset	1936-56	28	42	1	1428	105	34.82	1/9
T.J.Hearne	Berkshire	1922-23	8	11	0	132	31	12.00	-
H.M.Hinde	Berkshire	1921-32	34	41	16	103	20	4.12	-
H.B.Ilangaratne	Herts	2006-11	4	8	0	141	52	17.62	-/1
J.Johns	Glamorgan	1920	1	2	0	0	0	0.00	-
R.J.Richards	Essex II	1966-75	19	30	3	179	45	6.62	-
F.W.Wilkinson	Cambs	1923-48	76	106	11	1732	103	18.23	1/9

	B	M	R	W	BB	Ave	5i/10m	Ct/St
J.Coulthurst	799	34	402	26	5-65	15.46	1/-	1
M.N.Harbottle	48	0	34	1	1-24	34.00	-	12
T.J.Hearne	721	24	350	17	6-44	20.58	1/-	5
H.M.Hinde	4550	157	2323	153	8-78	15.18	12/3	15
H.B.Ilangaratne	-	-	-	-	-	-	-	1
J.Johns	24	0	16	0	-	-	-	0
R.J.Richards	-	-	-	-	-	-	-	22/4
F.W.Wilkinson	8998	313	4409	191	6-13	23.08	6/1	28

Note: The figures for Bob Richards are for appearances in the Second Eleven competition; all others are for appearances in the Minor Counties Championship.

Career records in other major competitions

Josiah Coulthurst in Lancashire League and Worsley Cup :

		M	I	NO	R	HS	Ave	100/50
East Lancashire	1914-32	122	38	458	21*	5.45	-/-	
	B	M	R	W	BB	Ave	5i	Ct/St
	10690	318	5039	390	8-14	12.92	25	37

Stuart Moffat in Scottish National Cricket League (Premier Division/Premiership):

		M	I	NO	R	HS	Ave	100/50
Grange	2000-11	55	48	10	1022	96	26.89	-/5
	B	M	R	W	BB	Ave	5i	Ct/St
	60	2	43	5	3-16	8.60	-	13

Principal career records in other sports

Jack Lee: Career in senior football

Team	Seasons	Football League		FA Cup		Other	
		Apps	Goals	Apps	Goals	Apps	Goals
Leicester City	1946/47-1949/50	123	74	14	10	-	-
Derby County	1950/51-1953/54	93	54	6	2	-	-
Coventry City	1954/55	15	8	3	2	-	-
England	1950/51	-	-	-	-	1	1
TOTAL		**231**	**136**	**23**	**14**	**1**	**1**

His full international was on 7 October 1950 v Northern Ireland at Windsor Road, Belfast when England won 4-1.

Stuart Moffat: Career in senior rugby union

Team	Seasons	Heineken Cup		Magners/ Celtic League		Internationals	
		Apps	Points	Apps	Points	Apps	Points
Glasgow Rugby	2002/03- 2003/04	9+1	0	18+1	30	-	-
Borders/Reivers	2004/05- 2006/07	8+2	60	43+4	25	-	-
Scotland	2002/03- 2004/05	-	-	-	-	3+1	5
TOTAL		**17+3**	**60**	**61+5**	**55**	**3+1**	**5**

Note: Figures after the '+' sign denote appearances as a replacement.

His four full internationals were: 9 November 2002 v Romania, played as full-back, scored one try, won 37-10; 16 November 2002 v South Africa, played as full-back, won 21-6; 24 November 2002 v Fiji, second-half replacement on the wing, won 36-22; 6 November 2004 v Australia, played as full-back, replaced at half-time, lost 14-31. All four matches were at Murrayfield, Edinburgh.

Index

The main subjects covered by this book are identified in bold type. A page number in bold indicates an illustration.